Inside Music

A Core Music Education Programme for children and young people aged 0 to 13

A Philosophy

'Inside Music' is based on the premise that children do not gather music from the air around them, but rather need a school music education programme which encompasses two key components - (i) 'curriculum music in class' and (ii) the 'extended music curriculum'. Both are essential to a balanced music education and, when working together, bring great benefits for pupils and the school.

Curriculum Music in Class

The proposition is that 'curriculum music' needs to be based upon a core programme which provides a carefully structured progression of learning, with continuity from year to year – a programme which helps each child, through good teaching, learning and performing in class, to acquire the skills and concepts needed for developing personal musicianship. This programme, therefore, provides continuity of learning from the Early Years Stage through to the end of Year 8 – the most effective age-range for music teaching and learning in a school classroom environment.

The content and structure of the 'Inside Music' Core Programme is designed (i) to be accessible to all children at each stage, (ii) to help teachers and schools to build a music curriculum which has immediate educational benefits as well as long-term sustainability, and (iii) to provide, for those who seek it, ongoing opportunities for an informed lifetime involvement in music.

Music-making

On its own, music-making does not necessarily result in music education; but, it is a key ingredient within any music education programme. If a carefully planned integration of musicianship development with music-making can be achieved, a progression of learning becomes possible which results in a deep understanding of music and a wide range of opportunities for children's personal achievement. The joy of making music is central to success in class music education and it is the teacher's responsibility to ensure that curriculum music opens the doors to further achievement for all in the 'extended music curriculum'.

The Extended Music Curriculum

The 'extended music curriculum' seeks to put into practice the musicianship acquired in class, according to each child's capabilities and levels of attainment. Consequently, the 'extended curriculum' takes the form of music-making and music performing beyond the classroom, into the school and the local community - often with the support of visiting teachers and other interested organisations.

The Two Performing Media in Music

'Inside Music' recognises that, for all modules of learning, there are two performing media in music – the singing voice and instruments. When the child uses his/her singing voice it is the child who makes the sound; a child makes no sound when using an instrument, but manipulates an object to make the sound. This is a significant distinction in music education. Therefore, the performing medium used by the teacher must be chosen for its effectiveness in achieving the learning outcome. This is a matter for the judgement of the teacher and 'Inside Music' is designed to offer guidance in this.

Michael Stocks

Published by The Voices Foundation
Copyright © The Voices Foundation

Acknowledgements

We are grateful to our colleagues below for supporting much of the preparatory work for this Early Years stage.

Team members:	Sarah Carling
	Ruth McCartney-Moore
	Andrew Maddocks
	Eleanor Duta
Listening materials:	Susan Hollingworth
	Naxos Licensing
Illustrations:	Chris Wright
CD Singer:	Jan Trott

We have made every effort to trace and acknowledge copyright owners. If any of them are not here, we offer our apologies and ask that you contact us immediately.

All the Little Ducks – words: Margaret Shephard

Easter Eggs: Lois Birkenshaw

Going on a picnic: Georgia E Garlid and Lynn Greeman Olson

I have sounds: Sue Nicholls

There's a spider on my toe: Sarah Carling

Where, oh where are all the babies?: Tamar Swade and Sheena Roberts

You are my sunshine: Jimmy Davies and Charles Mitchell

National Youth Choir of Scotland

Beth Hill

Michael Stocks

Published by The Voices Foundation
Copyright © The Voices Foundation

Inside Music

Early Years (Age 0 to 5 years)
A Music Education Programme for Early Years

Finding your way around the Early Years Module

This initial Module of 'Inside Music' provides a basis of experience upon which the progression and continuity of learning through Modules 1 to 4 can be built. In Early Years, the collection of carefully chosen songs and activities divides into sections representing the developmental stages of babies and young children, namely: Rocking, Looking and listening, Joining in, Finding those fingers and toes, Tickling, Up and about, Conversations, Curling and stretching, Playing with sounds, Signs and symbols, Circle games. Each section has an explanatory introduction. The layout is designed to help make the contents of the programme accessible and understandable for teachers and practitioners.

Attached CD

Each song is shown in staff notation and a track number is provided for those who wish to listen to the song on the attached CD. The words of the song are clearly shown on each page and, at the bottom of the page, a description of associated activities can be found. Some pages show a selection of attractive rhymes and chants to supplement the song collection.

On the same CD starting from Track 66, there is recommended listening material appropriate for children in this age-group. Notes on the listening material are found towards the end of this book.

(For simplification, 'he' and 'she' are used alternately for children of both sexes)

Reception Teachers

If you are teaching a Reception Class in school, this Early Years programme might be ideal for your children. If so, use it and enjoy the songs and rhymes.

However, some children might be ready to move on by beginning to learn some of the basic skills and concepts for early musicianship (for example, rhythm, heartbeat, phrase, etc.). If this is the case, we recommend that you obtain Module 1 of 'Inside Music' which will give you a framework for ongoing teaching and learning.

Musical Play Time

After songs are led by the practitioner, let there be time and a place for children to sing by themselves or with friends. Maybe leave out the puppets and other resources (see page 6). Lucky bag cards can be used for this too (see pages 111-122).

Published by The Voices Foundation
Copyright © The Voices Foundation

Contents

Introduction	5
Rocking	9
Looking and listening	17
Joining in	25
Finding those fingers and toes	41
Tickling	47
Up and about	51
Conversations	59
Curling and stretching	67
Playing with sounds	75
Signs and symbols	87
Circle games	91
Listening material	101
Songs grouped by activity	106
A-Z indexes of rhymes and songs	107
Skills and concepts	109
Listening material tracks	110
'Lucky bag' cards	111

Published by The Voices Foundation
Copyright © The Voices Foundation

Early Years Stage

Introduction

Babies listen, babies respond, babies use their singing voice before they talk. Singing and talking to a new-born baby in a gentle, cooing voice, with faces very close together, comes naturally to many parents and carers. Think of the passer-by who puts her head inside the pram and says in a lilting, high-pitched voice, "Hello, aren't you a pretty girl then?" This may sound foolish to some adults, but the baby will listen and respond to the singing voice, and enjoy the closeness and the eye-contact.

The world of sound is all around them, and from an early age, they will respond with pleasure to a singing voice. Of course when the first 'singing' noise is made, the child who receives a delighted response from a nearby adult will soon understand that this is a sound which should be repeated. And so singing begins.

For parents and carers, music-making is one of the best ways to build a relationship with their child. Known songs can provide opportunities for dialogue and for establishing routines. So building a repertoire of simple songs is crucial. Both songs and rhymes can be sung in the child's home language. Adults who know lots of songs and rhymes can sing themselves out of some tricky situations !! Music can be used to calm or to stimulate.

Clapping games, rhymes and singing games from all around the world have been passed down through generations. Children love rhymes and songs that are easy to sing, have strong rhythms, amusing vocabulary, and a regular pulse. Young children crave the opportunity to sing and speak, and this helps them make good relationships both with adults and their peer group. It also prepares them for conversational skills.

In addition to specific musical skills (see page 109) the songs and rhymes in this book will develop skills of the whole child. For example:

- memory
- intellectual skills
- emotional and social skills
- speech and language
- listening skills and concentration
- good behaviour patterns
- physical coordination

> "Babies respond differently to different sounds and from an early age are able to distinguish sound patterns. They learn to talk by being talked to. Babies and children use their voices to make contact and to let people know what they need and how they feel, establishing their own identities and personalities".

This quotation is from 'Communication, Language and Literacy' at
www.nationalstrategies.standards.dcsf.gov.uk/node/132712
(accessed 2 December 2010).

Children's voices

Pre-school children have a limited range of notes that they can sing accurately. Many of the songs in this book are appropriate for small children to sing at pitch. You don't need to stick to the key that they are written in, but remember that young children talk and sing at a higher pitch than adults. There are also songs with wider pitch ranges. Sing them to children, but don't always expect that they will sing too.

Improvising

Improvising with a baby can start at a very early age. When the first cooing noises begin, the baby will enjoy the physical sensation when you copy and match the pitch of the sound. Continue to do this as he gets older and begins to make proper words. Make your voice go up and down as you pretend to be in a rocket with the small child on your knee, going higher and lower with your voice and the actions. Make whizzing/ brmming noises as you push the buggy along the street. Take a tune you know well and improvise some new words to it. Sing as you lay the table, tidy up, climb the stairs ("This is the way we climb the stairs…")

There are many songs in the book which give opportunities for improvising. The more you try it, the easier it will become. After a while you will begin to do it instinctively. So will the child! You can't always find the song to suit the occasion, so make one up.

Movement

Rocking comes naturally to many people who hold a baby in their arms. As the baby grows, so does the movement. Children are rarely still except when they sleep. Holding hands and swaying from side to side, jumping up and down as you sing, humming and listening to music are lovely feelings for a small child. Use the listening ideas to move to the pulse of the music, following the movements made by the child. Wave coloured scarves over your head. Give out soft toys or puppets and tap them on the floor to the beat. This will also help with fine motor skills. Many of the songs in the book have actions which go with them, increasing awareness of the pulse, rhythm and metre (strong and weak beats) of the song.

Resources

Some of the songs and rhymes in the book suggest the use of different resources. You don't need to spend a great deal of money. Here is a list of things which you will find useful when singing with individuals, small or larger groups:

Puppets and soft toys

These attract instant attention and will encourage good listening. A hand puppet with a moving mouth will make the children pay close attention. The puppet can make deliberate mistakes and you can encourage the children to correct them. Finger puppets and soft toys can be handed out to children for call and response singing. Pop up puppets are useful for showing children higher and lower (Jack in the box, page 69) or for encouraging them to sing in their 'thinking voice' when the puppet hides (Twinkle, twinkle, little star, page 88).

Crushed velvet blanket

Buy a metre and a half of blue lycra or stretchy velvet. This can be used for many songs; it makes a marvellous pond to put fish or frogs on, or a child can be invited to hide underneath while you sing a peek-a-boo song.

Published by The Voices Foundation
Copyright © The Voices Foundation

Instruments

You can use many body parts to create instrumental sounds: clapping, slapping, stamping, clicking fingers. Kitchen utensils can be turned into instant percussion instruments, spoons, pots and boxes with dried goods in etc. Make sure you supervise the use of these though. When you move on to real percussion instruments remember that one good quality instrument is worth several poor plastic toy ones. Children will always love the sound of a drum and enjoy having the opportunity to play it. (Listen, listen, here I come, page 83, The drums in the band, page 80.) When working with a group show a few instruments and pass them around between songs so that the children get to experience the timbre of each different one. Keep the songs short so that they all get a turn. This will work much better (and you are less likely to get a headache!) than giving everyone an instrument and getting them to bang together. Allow a few children to play them while everyone else sings, and a sense of pulse will begin to emerge.

Chiffon scarves

Small children love to hide their faces under scarves that they can still see through. Their attention span will increase as you sing a whole song, and they wait in suspense until the last "peek-a-boo" phrase. (Songs on pages 35-37.) Scarves can also be used to move to the pulse of music. Extend their use for dancing in a slow and smooth way. Children find it difficult to move slowly so the scarves will help them. Use the listening tracks.

Magic box or lucky bag

Put the session's props into a pretty box and sing "Magic box, magic box, what's in my magic box?" before each song. The children will love to open it and take out a puppet or picture. Or print out and laminate the lucky dip cards and put them in a drawstring bag for the same purpose (a master of which is on the CD supplied, with a hard copy at the back of the book).

Beth Hill

Published by The Voices Foundation
Copyright © The Voices Foundation

Rocking

Rocking a baby and singing gentle songs to lull him to sleep is a practice which has been used throughout the ages and in all cultures. A simple made-up melody with repetitive words, whilst rocking from side to side, is known to be reassuring and settling. The baby will associate the song with going to sleep (especially if it is the same song every time). Older children too will enjoy the feeling of security that the song and the rocking movement bring.

Bye baby bunting

TRACK 4

Bye baby bunting,
Daddy's gone a-hunting.
Gone to catch a rabbit skin
To wrap poor baby bunting in.
Bye baby bunting.

Bye ba-by bunt-ing, Dad-dy's gone a hunt-ing. Gone to catch a rab-bit skin to wrap poor ba-by bunt-ing in. Bye ba-by bunt-ing,

Sing to your tiny baby, rocking from side to side with the pulse. This is an easy tune for an older child to sing whilst rocking a teddy or a doll.

Sleep baby sleep

TRACK 49

Sleep baby sleep
Father tends the sheep,
Mother shakes the dreamland tree
And down come all the dreams for thee,
Sleep baby sleep.

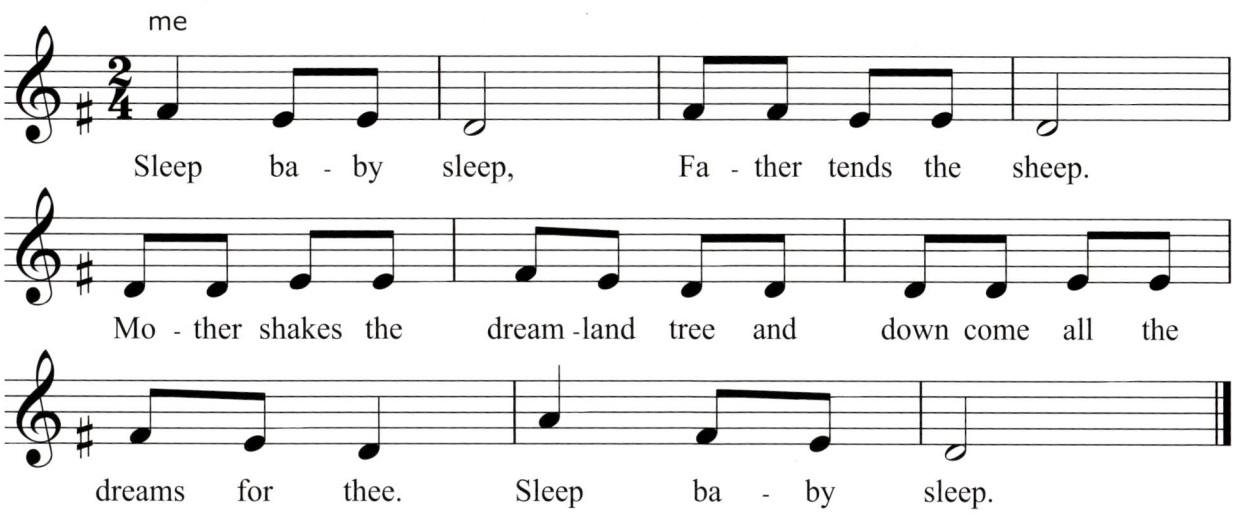

This is a beautiful song from Germany. Why not begin with slightly louder singing and gradually get quieter - finishing by whispering. Encourage three to five year olds to sing quietly once their teddy is 'asleep'.

Suogân

TRACK 50

Suogân, do not weep,
Suogân, go to sleep.
Suogân, have no fear,
Suogân, mother's near.

Su - o - gân, do not weep, Su - o - gân, go to sleep.
Su - o - gân, have no fear, Su - o - gân, mo - ther's near.

This is a traditional Welsh lullaby. Pronounce it "See-oh-gahn". It is a good song for slow rocking movements. It may be easier to perform this while standing.

Published by The Voices Foundation
Copyright © The Voices Foundation

Lullaby my baby

TRACK 34

Lullaby my baby,
Softly sleeps my child.
Sister quietly rocks you,
Light her hands and mild.

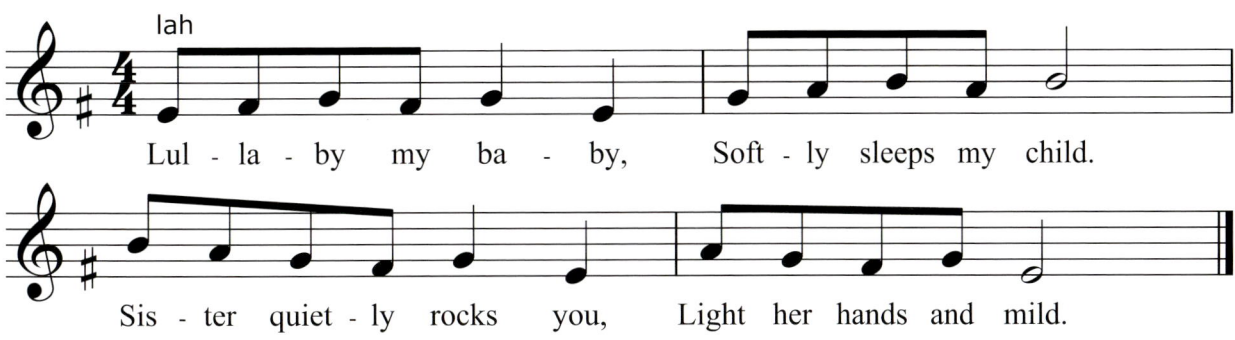

Traditional Latvian. Substitute baby's name for the word "baby". Holding the baby close, hum gently. The baby will feel the music as well as hearing it.

Hari coo coo

TRACK 15

Hari coo coo, Yari coo coo,
Yari coo coo a lay.
Hari coo coo, Yari coo coo,
Hari coo coo a lay.
(Repeat)

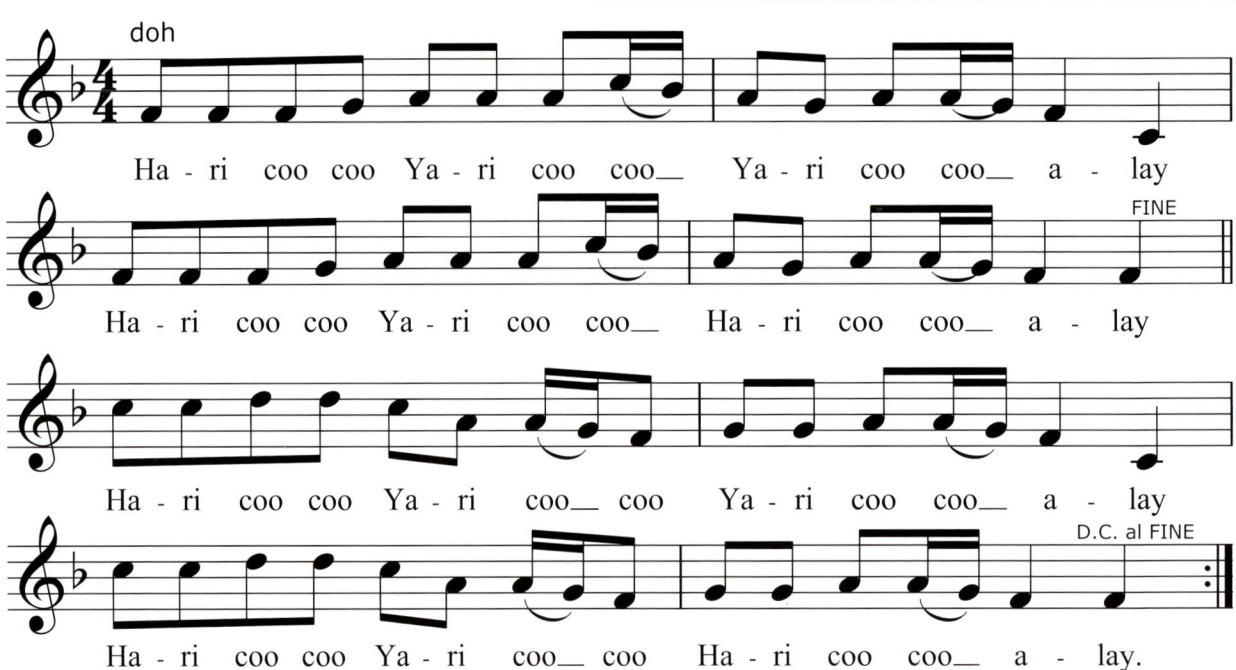

An Indian lullaby. Let the baby see your face as you sing. Play with the words and exaggerate your mouth shape on "coo coo". Encourage playful imitation.

Ally bally bee

TRACK 3

Ally bally, ally bally bee,
Sittin' on your mammy's knee,
Greetin' for anither bawbee
Tae buy mair Coulter's Candy.

Al - ly bal - ly al - ly bal - ly bee,
Sit - tin' on your mam - my's knee,
Greet - in' for an - i - ther baw - bee tae
buy mair Coul - ter's Can - dy.

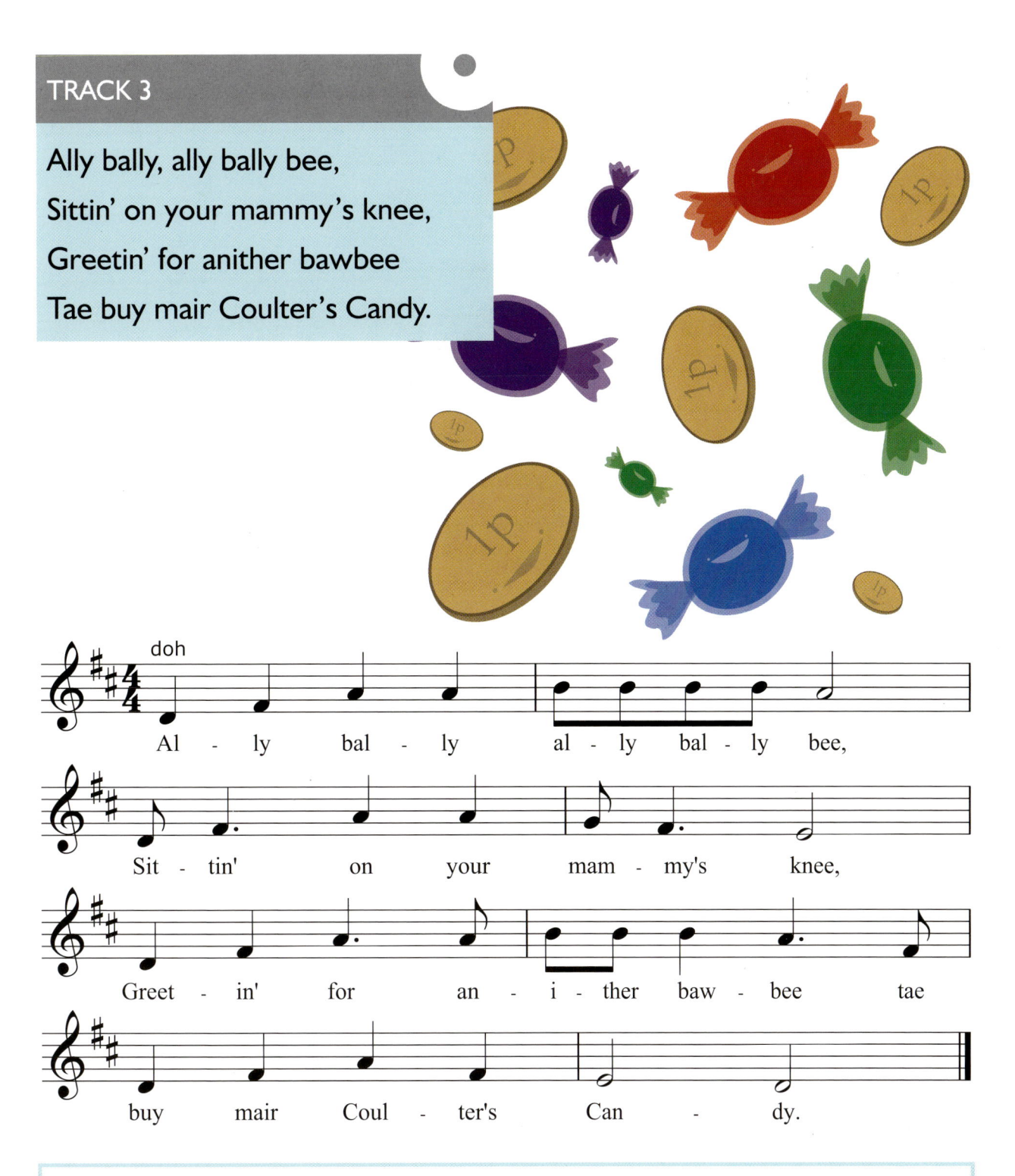

This is a Scottish song. "Greetin'" means "crying". "Anither bawbee" means "another penny" as a child asks for money to buy Coulter's Candy (sweets).

Allundé

TRACK 2

Allundé, allundé
Allundé, alluya.
Allundé, allundé
Allundé, alluya.

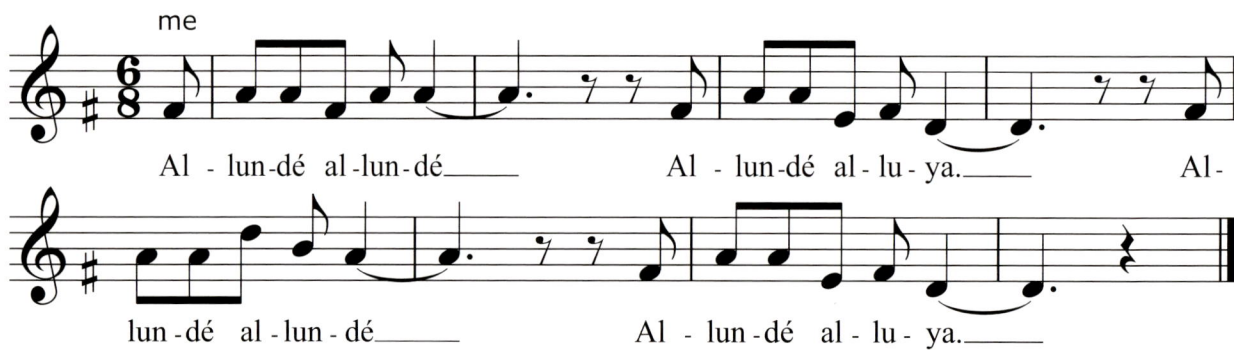

A traditional East African lullaby which has a beautiful rocking pulse.

Looking and listening

Singing to a young baby will help her respond to a range of familiar sounds, and very quickly she will turn to the voice and respond with pleasure. Croon to the tiniest babies. Sing as you change a nappy or get her dressed. Let the song reflect what you are doing. The baby will not mind if you don't sing in tune, or your voice is not as lovely as you want it to be.

Hush little baby

TRACK 22

Hush little baby, don't say a word,
Daddy's gonna buy you a mocking bird.
And if that mocking bird don't sing,
Daddy's gonna buy you a diamond ring.
And if that diamond ring turns to brass,
Daddy's gonna buy you a looking glass.
And if that looking glass gets broke,
Daddy's gonna buy you a billy goat.
And if that billy goat runs away,
Daddy's gonna buy you another today.

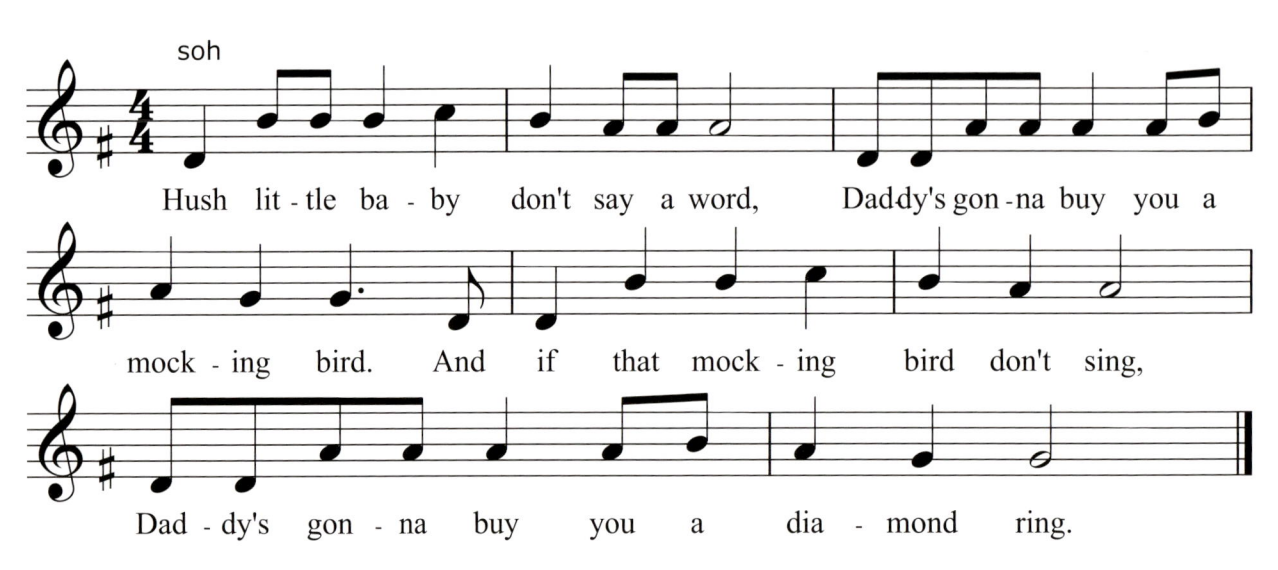

This is a very old, traditional American song. Many generations have sung it and parents still enjoy singing it to the youngest children in their families.

You are my sunshine

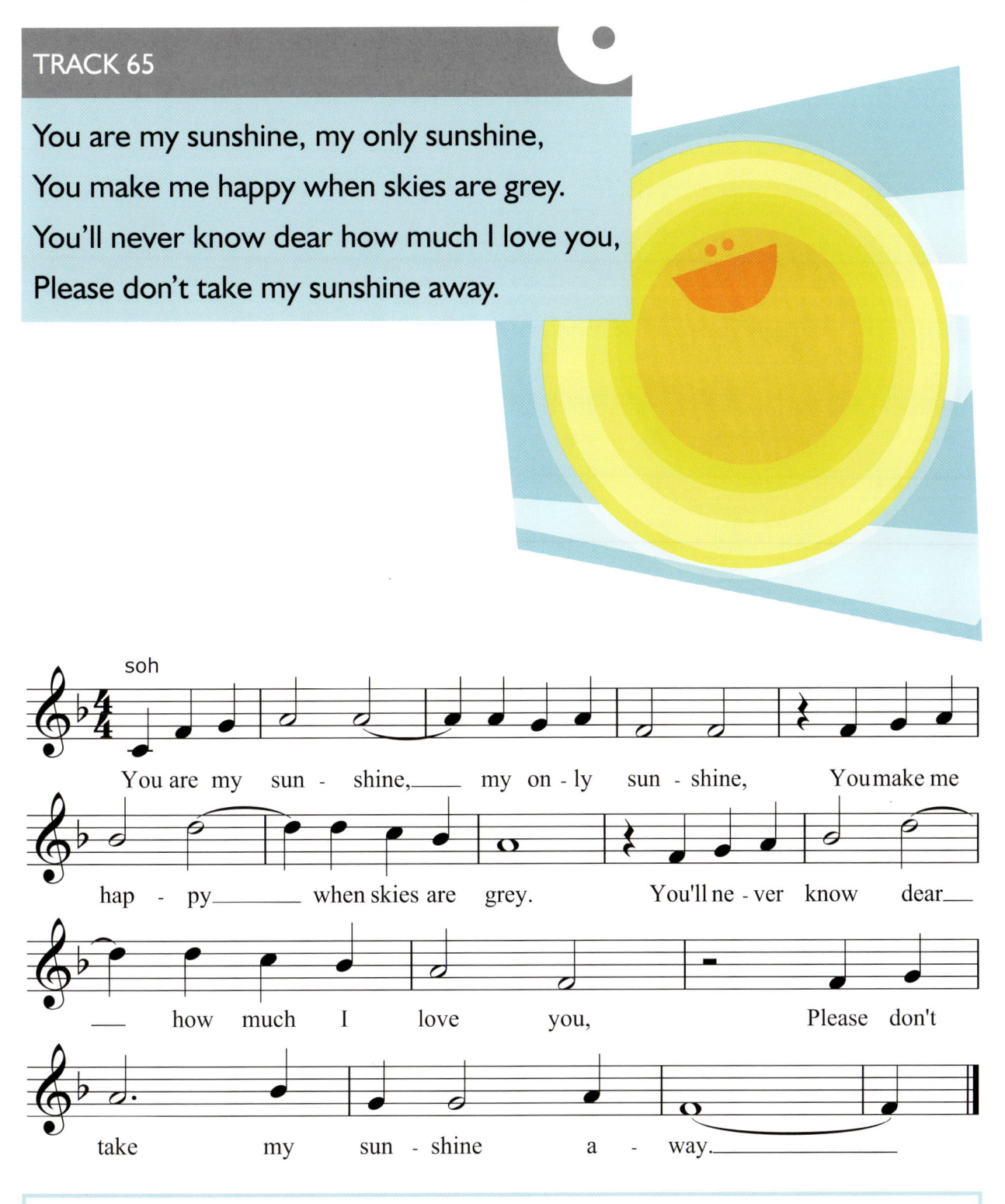

TRACK 65

You are my sunshine, my only sunshine,
You make me happy when skies are grey.
You'll never know dear how much I love you,
Please don't take my sunshine away.

This is a lovely song with long, soothing phrases – good for settling a child.

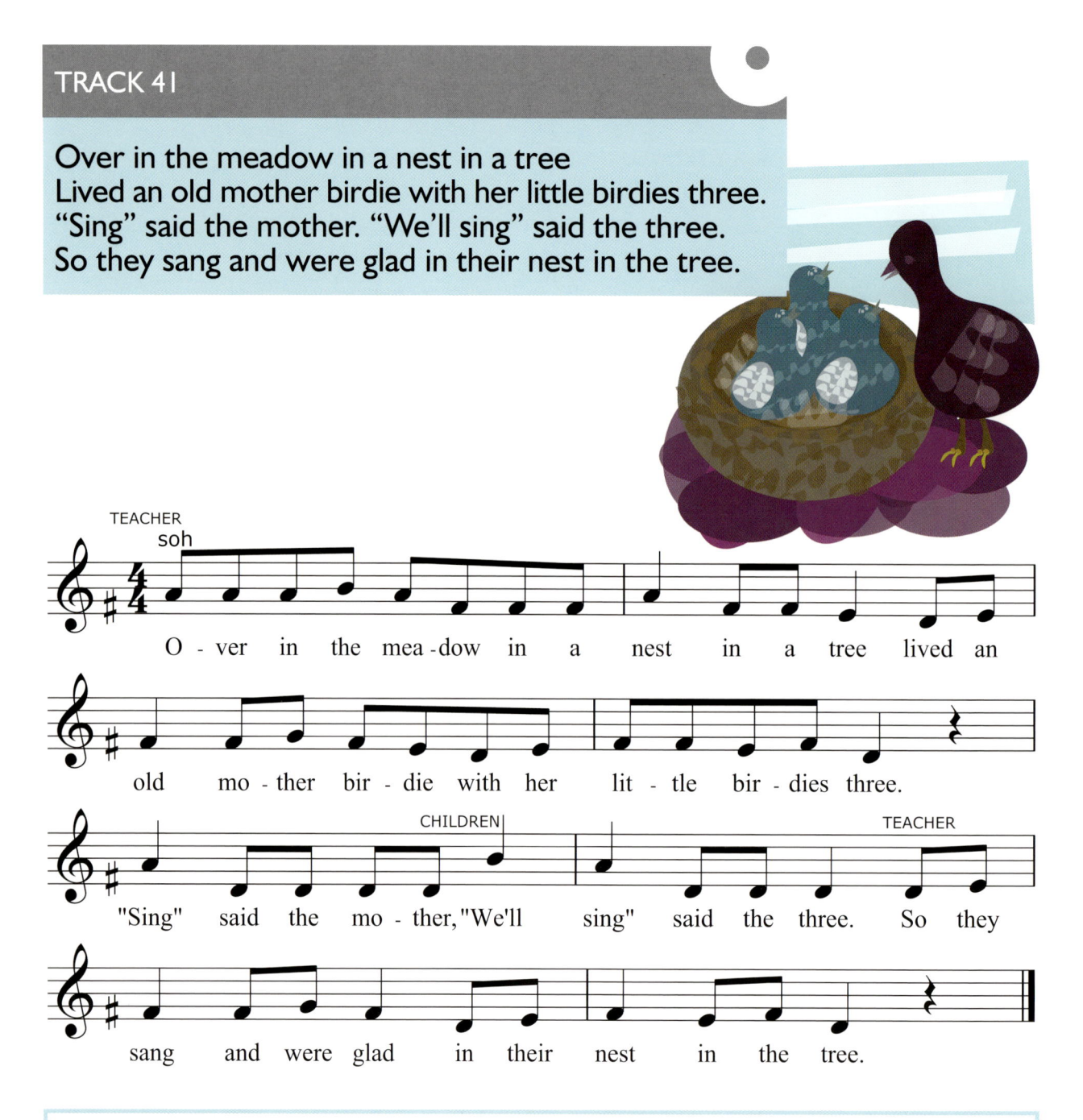

Over in the meadow

TRACK 41

Over in the meadow in a nest in a tree
Lived an old mother birdie with her little birdies three.
"Sing" said the mother. "We'll sing" said the three.
So they sang and were glad in their nest in the tree.

TEACHER
soh

O-ver in the mea-dow in a nest in a tree lived an old mo-ther bir-die with her lit-tle bir-dies three.

CHILDREN   TEACHER

"Sing" said the mo-ther, "We'll sing" said the three. So they sang and were glad in their nest in the tree.

You can add your own verses to this song, for example:
Over in the meadow in a pond in the sun, lived an old mother duck and her little duck one…
Over in the meadow in a stream so blue, lived an old mother fishie and her little fishies two…
Involve children in making up their own verses.

Lavender's blue

TRACK 30

Lavender's blue, dilly, dilly, lavender's green.

When I am king, dilly, dilly, you shall be queen.

Call up your men, dilly, dilly, set them to work.

Some to the plough, dilly, dilly, some to the cart.

Some to make hay, dilly, dilly, some to cut corn.

While you and I, dilly, dilly keep ourselves warm.

A traditional English love song with a beautiful melody, sung by generations of family members.

Pitter patter

TRACK 44

Pitter patter, pitter patter, listen to the rain.
Pitter patter, pitter patter, on the window pane.

Splishy sploshy, splishy sploshy,
I am getting wet,
Splishy sploshy, splishy sploshy,
Raindrops on my head.

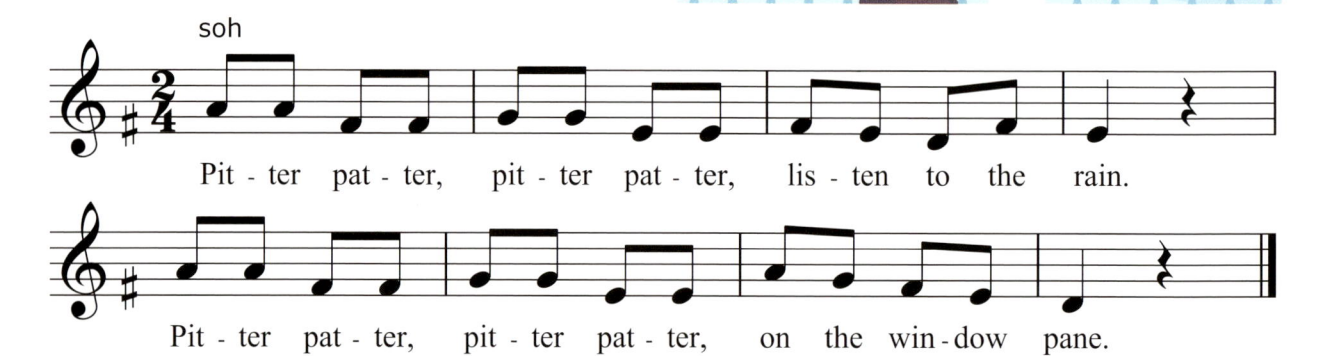

Sing the first verse while looking out of the window; sing the second verse when you are outside! It's also fun to sing this song at bath time or when you are playing with water.

What shall we do when the baby cries?

TRACK 58

What shall we do when the baby cries?
What shall we do when the baby cries?
Wrap him up in calico,
Send him to his daddy-oh.
Rock a bye the baby,
Rock a bye the baby oh,
Rock a bye the baby,
Rock a bye the baby oh.

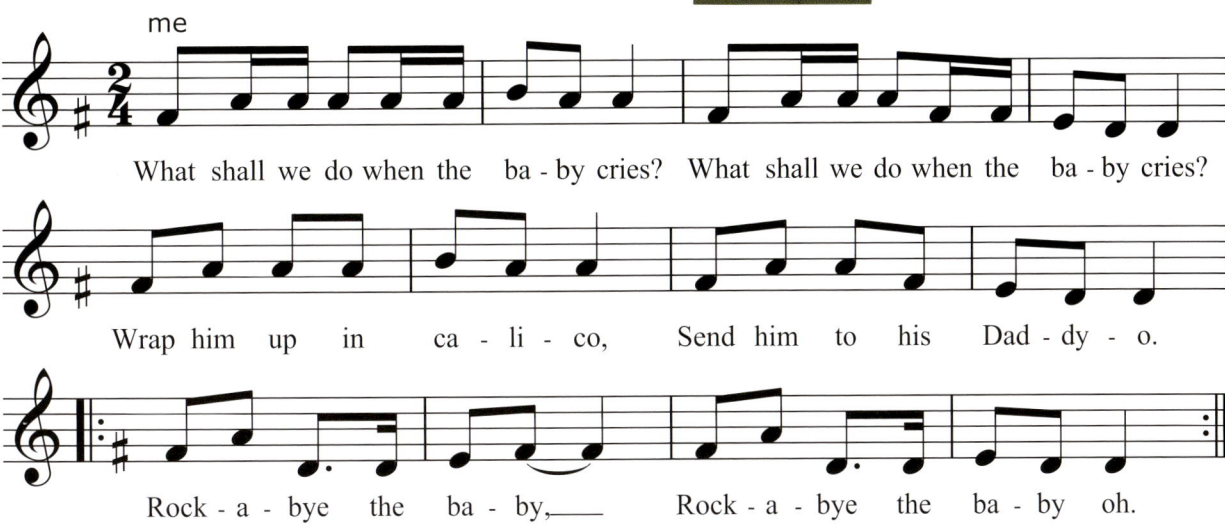

A lovely bouncy song to enjoy with your baby. An older child might even sing it to a favourite teddy bear or doll. Smile as you rock the baby or swing his arms in time with the pulse.

Published by The Voices Foundation
Copyright © The Voices Foundation

Joining in

Small children love repetition and take pleasure in making and listening to a wide variety of sounds. Listen to the sound your baby makes, and copy it at the same pitch. Sing the same songs again and again to small children and very soon they will anticipate and join in with the final word of each phrase. Encourage them to join in, and when they do, match your voice to theirs. Singing songs which involve repetition and rhyme also helps with language acquisition and eventually, reading. Peek-a-boo games can be used when getting dressed: "Where is Lily's hand, wish I knew. Boo!".

Five little monkeys

TRACK 13

Singing voice
Five little monkeys sitting in a tree,
Whispering voice
Along comes Mister Crocodile as quiet as can be,
Singing voice
Hey Mister Crocodile you can't catch me.
Shouting voice
SNAP!

Four little monkeys…(etc.)

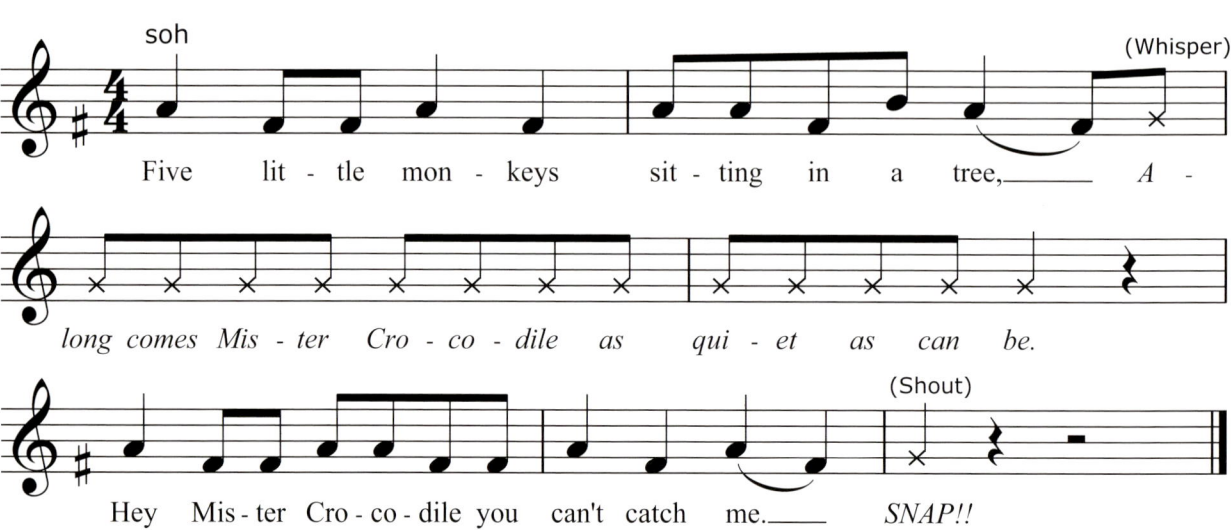

Five lit-tle mon-keys sit-ting in a tree,___ A-long comes Mis-ter Cro-co-dile as qui-et as can be. Hey Mis-ter Cro-co-dile you can't catch me.___ SNAP!!

Younger children will enjoy the anticipation before you say "SNAP!" Use the song to focus older children's attention and encourage them to move together on the word "SNAP!" This song can also be used to practise counting backwards (four little monkeys… etc).

Published by The Voices Foundation
Copyright © The Voices Foundation

Old MacDonald had a farm

TRACK 38

Old MacDonald had a farm. EIEIO.
And on that farm he had some cows. EIEIO.
With a moo moo here and a moo moo there.
Here a moo, there a moo,
Everywhere a moo moo.
Old MacDonald had a farm. EIEIO.

The animal noises are particularly good for promoting vowel sounds to develop language – ah-ay-ee-aw-oo. Suitable animal sounds might be: sheep (baa), horses (neigh), donkeys (ee-aw) and cows (moo).

Published by The Voices Foundation
Copyright © The Voices Foundation

Pease pudding hot

TRACK 42

Pease pudding hot,

Pease pudding cold,

Pease pudding in the pot nine days old.

Some like it hot,

Some like it cold,

Some like it in the pot nine days old.

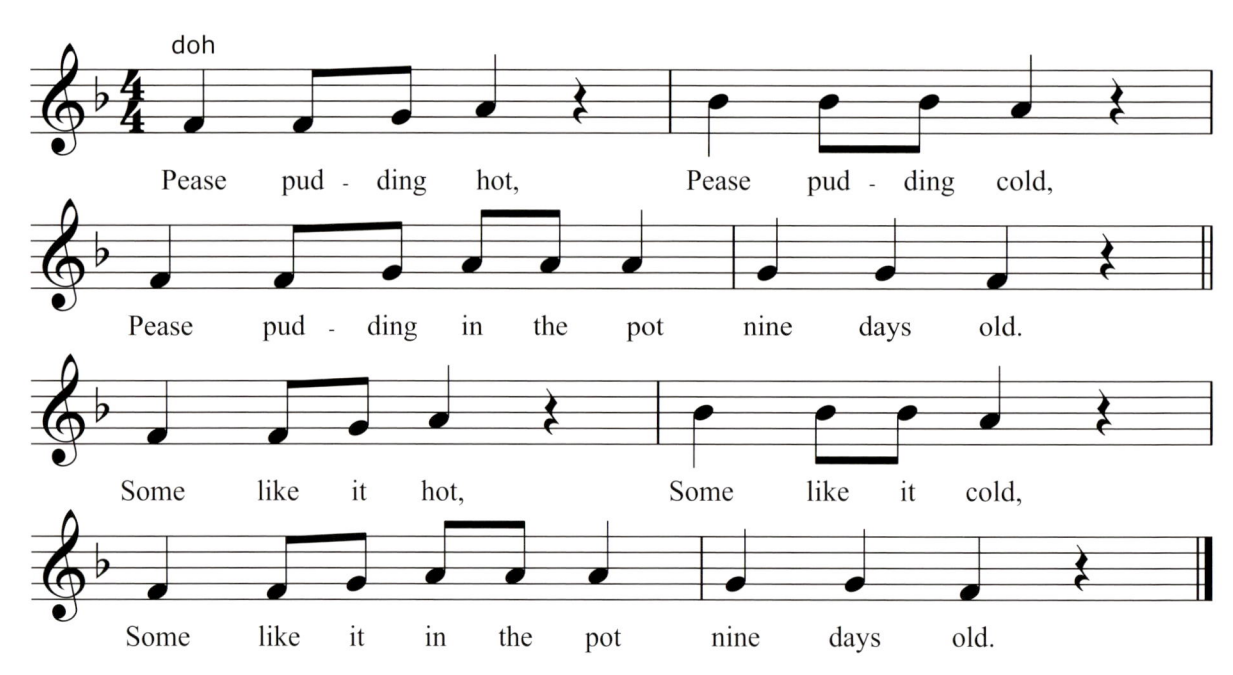

Children will love to do the actions to this song. Wipe your brow or blow at the end of the first phrase, shiver and hold your arms in the second, and make a horrid face after "nine days old". As the children gain confidence, ask them to take turns – some children singing and some performing the actions. Ask a confident child to perform the actions or to sing on their own.

Published by The Voices Foundation
Copyright © The Voices Foundation

There's a spider on my toe

TRACK 54

There's a spider on my toe,
There's a spider on my toe,
Oh no! Oh no!
There's a spider on my toe.

There's a spider on my knee…oh gee…
There's a spider on my tum…oh mum…
There's a spider on my head…oh dread…

Aaaachoo!!!
There's a spider on the floor…
He's not on me any more…

(melody line, starting on soh, 4/4)
There's a spi-der on my toe, there's a spi-der on my toe.
Oh, no! Oh, no! There's a spi-der on my toe.

Start by tapping a puppet on your toe, in time with the pulse as you sing. For further verses encourage children to find new body parts and maybe even a rhyme to fit. There are three ideas above – knee, tum and head. You could also make a swooping sound as the spider gradually moves up the body.

"Mm, mm," went the little green frog

TRACK 53

"Mm, mm," went the little green frog one day.
"Mm, mm," went the little green frog.
"Mm, mm," went the little green frog one day.
And the frog said "Mm, mm, whaa".
But we know frogs go
(clap) "La di da di da, *(flap hands to the side)*
(clap) La di da di da,
(clap) La di da di da".
We know frogs go *(clap)* "La di da di da,"
They don't go, "Mm, mm whaa."

Stick your tongue out on the first "mm" and hum on the second. Maintain good eye contact with younger children to encourage them to copy.

Incey Wincey spider

TRACK 25

Incey Wincey spider climbed up the water spout.

Down came the rain and washed the spider out.

Out came the sun and dried up all the rain,

So Incey Wincey spider climbed up the spout again.

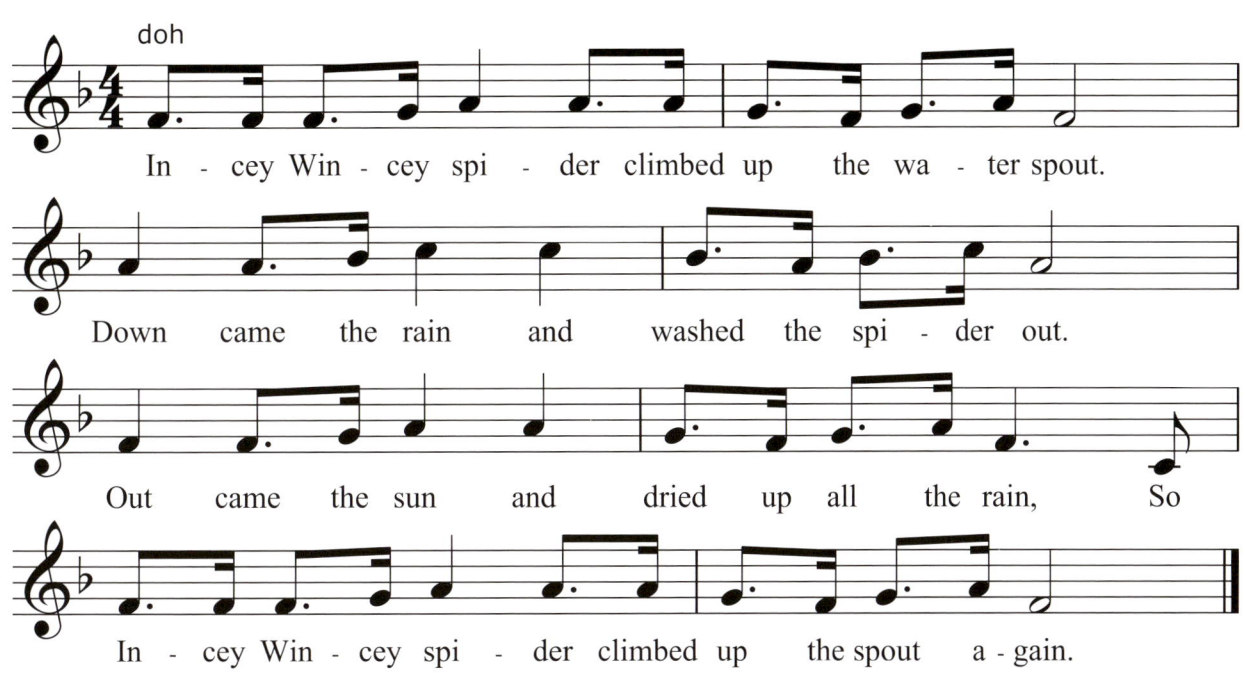

In - cey Win - cey spi - der climbed up the wa - ter spout.

Down came the rain and washed the spi - der out.

Out came the sun and dried up all the rain, So

In - cey Win - cey spi - der climbed up the spout a - gain.

A traditional action song which everyone knows and children love. Use your own actions as you sing the song.

Clap, clap, clap your hands

TRACK 7

Clap, clap, clap your hands,
Clap your hands together.

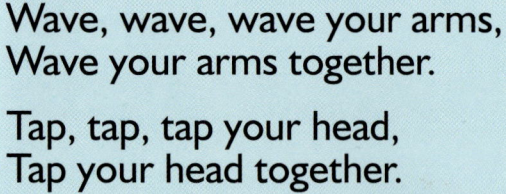

Wave, wave, wave your arms,
Wave your arms together.

Tap, tap, tap your head,
Tap your head together.

Try using this song for 'lining up' before going outside, or for other daily routines. The children can choose the actions.

Ickle ockle, blue bottle

TRACK 23

Ickle ockle, blue bottle,
Fishes in the sea.
If you want a partner
Just choose me!

Ic - kle, oc - kle, blue bot - tle, fish - es in the sea.
If you want a part - ner just choose me!

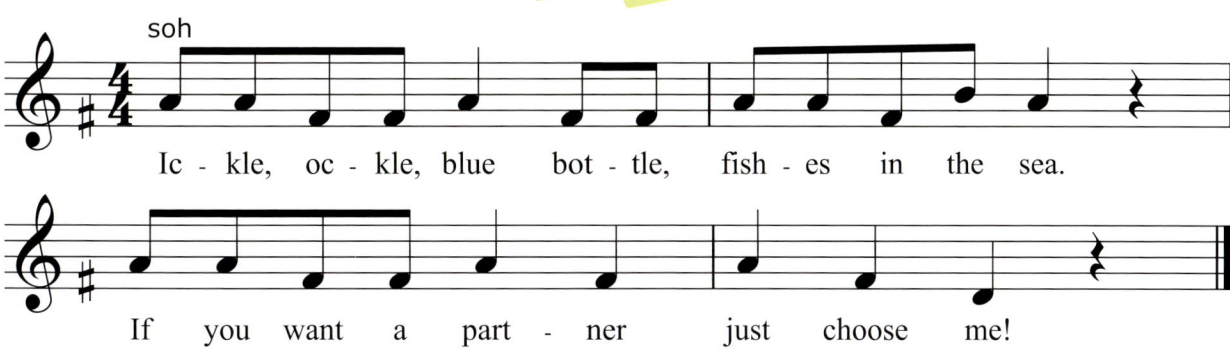

You can play this as a partner game. Form a circle; a selected child walks round inside the circle and chooses a clapping partner (an eager singer maybe!). Sing the song again while the pair clap each other's hands and then their own knees in time with the pulse. Alternatively, sing the song a second time while the pair dance together in the middle.

Easter eggs

TRACK 12

Easter eggs, Easter eggs, yellow, green and blue.

Easter eggs, Easter eggs, one for me and you.

Easter eggs, Easter eggs, yellow, blue and green

Easter eggs, Easter eggs, prettiest I have seen.

If you wish, change the song words to match the colours on your own decorated Easter eggs - for example: red, white and blue; then purple, pink and green. In time with the pulse, older children might pat a wooden egg or an egg shaker on the palm of the hand.

Little baby, fast asleep

TRACK 32

Little baby *(use child's name)* fast asleep,
Little baby, do not peek.
Little baby, where are you?
Little baby, peek-a-boo!

Peek-a-boo is a well established game that all babies love. It is a long time for the baby to wait until the last phrase, so be playful with your hands over your eyes during the first three phrases. Older children might hide their faces under chiffon scarves.

Where, oh where are all the babies?

TRACK 63

Where, oh where are all the babies?
Where have they gone? BOO!
Where, oh where are all the babies?
Where have they gone? BOO!

[Musical score: soh, 4/4 time, in G major]

Where, oh where are all the ba-bies? Where have they gone? BOO!
Where, oh where are all the ba-bies? Where have they gone? BOO!

Give each child a chiffon scarf to place over their head. This is good for concentration as they should last until "BOO!". For extra fun, 'hide' children under a large blanket or parachute material.

Where is Georgie?

татACK 62

Where is Georgie?
(use child's name)

Wish I knew.

Pull down the scarf and

PEEK-A-BOO!

Where is Geor-gie? Wish I knew. Pull down the scarf and PEEKA BOO!

Singing to each child in turn, 'hide' the child under a light see-through chiffon scarf until they are revealed.

Joining-in rhymes

Rhymes are just as important as songs – very useful in lots of situations and you won't have to remember the tune! Here are six we really like!

As children get older, try pausing just before the last word of each phrase – an excellent way to encourage them to join in!

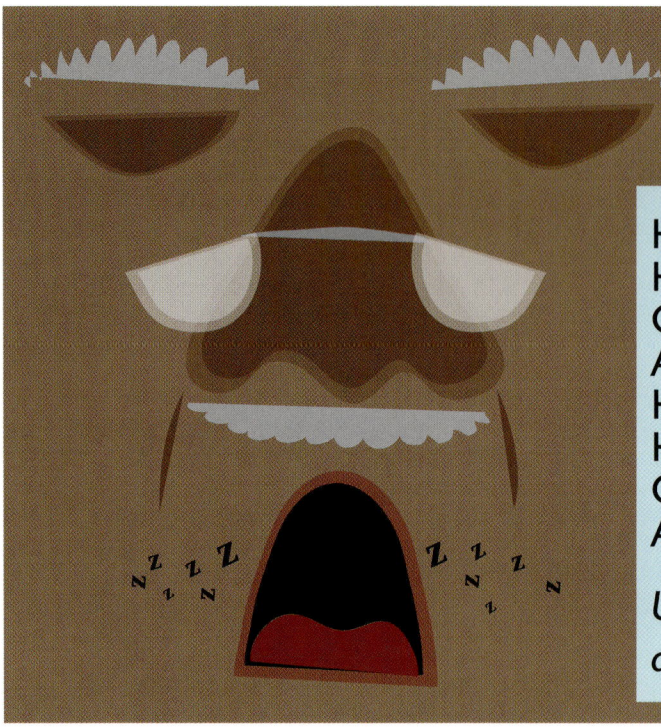

Here are grandma's glasses,
Here is grandma's hat.
Grandma claps her hands like this
And folds them in her lap.
Here are grandad's glasses,
Here is grandad's hat.
Grandad folds his arms like this
And has a little nap.

Use different voices for "grandma" and "grandad", and add actions.

Five fat sausages
sizzling in a pan.
All of a sudden one
went BANG!

Stay very still during the rhyme, and then clap or make another loud noise on "BANG!"

Published by The Voices Foundation
Copyright © The Voices Foundation

More joining-in rhymes

Swing me over the ocean, swing me over the sea,
Swing me over the garden wall and swing me home for tea!

Rock a small baby, and for older children be a bit more energetic with your swinging!

Mum and Dad and Uncle John
Got on the pony and rode along.
Dad fell off .... Weeeeee
Mum fell off ....Weeeeee
But Uncle John rode ....
on and on and on and on ....

A bouncing rhyme with lots of 'falling over' and fun.

More joining-in rhymes

Ha ha ha, hee hee hee,
Three little monkeys up a tree,
One fell down (weeeeeee) and hurt his knee,
Ha ha ha, hee hee hee.

… Two little monkeys…
…One little monkey…

Last verse

Ha ha ha, hee hee hee,
No little monkeys up a tree,
They've all gone home for their tea,
Ha ha ha, hee hee hee.

Apples, peaches, pears and plums,
Tell me when your birthday comes.
January, February, March…
(Stop on child's birthday)

Bounce a baby on your lap, then lift him high on his birthday month. An older child can clap or jump – good for autumn-born children!

Finding those fingers and toes

Children's responses develop as they learn to anticipate and join in with finger and word play. It also increases their attention span, as they enjoy feeling you moving their fingers and toes. They might begin to do it themselves. The songs and rhymes will help older children to count backwards and forwards.

Magic fingers

TRACK 35

Magic fingers hide away,
How many fingers come to play?
(Five) fingers come to play.

soh
Ma - gic fin - gers hide a - way,
How ma - ny fin - gers come to play?
(Five) fin - gers come to play.

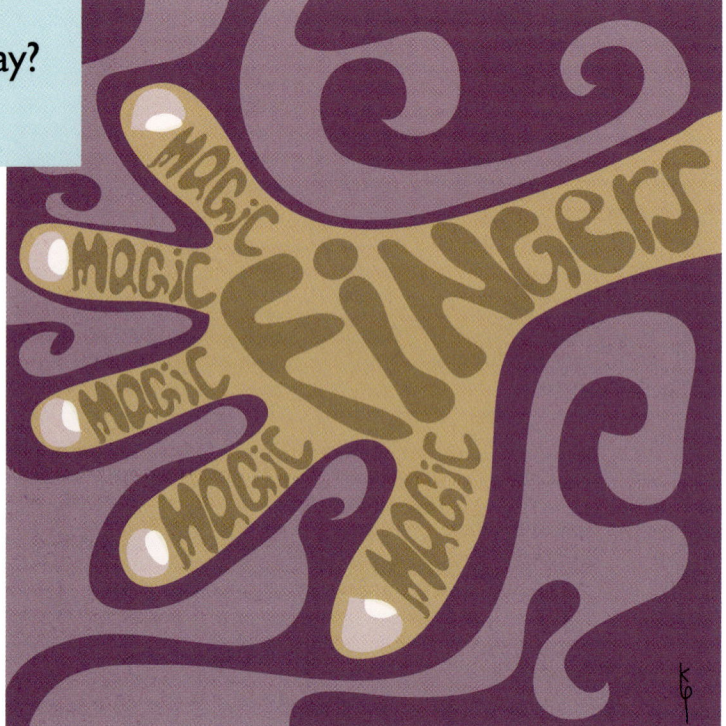

Wiggle your fingers at the beginning of the song. Then hide them behind your back, before revealing them and asking the children to count how many fingers are being held up. After some practice, a child might be selected to lead the song.

Published by The Voices Foundation
Copyright © The Voices Foundation

All the little ducks

TRACK 1

All the little ducks turn upside down,
Upside down, upside down.
All the little ducks turn upside down.
When they dabble at the bottom of the pond.

All the little beaks go quack quack quack…

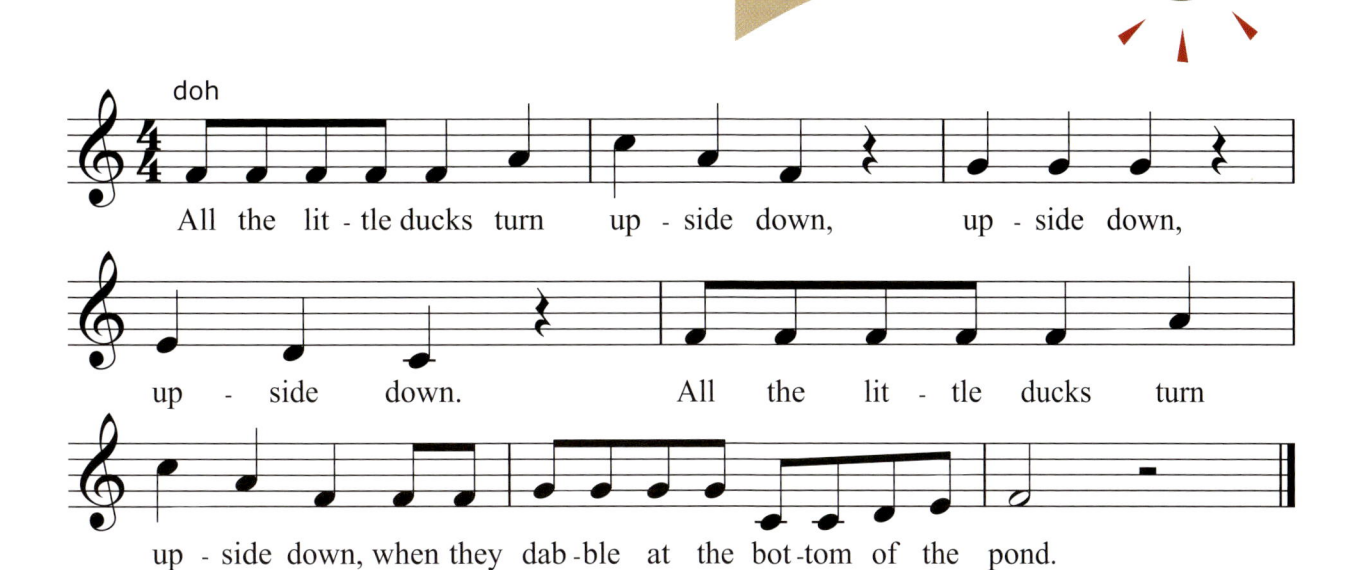

All the little tails go wiggle waggle wiggle…

Put up two thumbs to represent the ducks. Turn them over with the words of the song. Make a quacking shape with your hand for verse 2 and put your hands together and wiggle for verse 3.

Finger rhymes

One potato,
Two potato,
Three potato,
Four,
Five potato,
Six potato,
Seven potato,
More.

Make fists and place one on top of the other in turn, climbing and keeping the beat.

Roly poly roly poly, up, up, up.
Roly poly roly poly, down, down, down.
Roly poly roly poly, hands behind your back.
Roly poly roly poly, put them in your lap.

If you swap the last two lines, then you can play peek-a-boo! at the end. But if you need the children to be quiet, stick to the original way!

Two little dickie birds sitting on a wall,
One named Peter and one named Paul.
Fly away Peter, fly away Paul,
Come back Peter, come back Paul.

Follow the actions with your index fingers. Use finger puppets, or draw a face on a sticker to attach to the end of your finger.

Fingers like to wiggle waggle right in front of me,
Fingers like to wiggle waggle then fall on my knee.

Other verses - Wave up high, Curl up small, Stand up straight

Published by The Voices Foundation
Copyright © The Voices Foundation

More finger rhymes

Five little peas in a pea pod pressed.
(clench fists)
One grew, two grew, so did all the rest.
(open out the fingers, one at a time)
They grew and they grew and they did not stop
(open and shut hand)
Until one day the pod went POP!
(clap on the final word)

Try this with a piece of stretchy fabric; pull it out slowly and let it go on "POP!"

Johnny Johnny
Johnny Johnny
Whoops Johnny
Whoops Johnny
Johnny Johnny
Johnny!

Starting with little finger, touch each finger in turn sliding between index finger and thumb saying "whoops". You can also use a child's name.

Here is the beehive
but where are all the bees?
Hiding away where nobody sees.
Here come the bees now
Out of the hive!
1,2,3,4,5 bzzzzzzzz!

Hide 5 fingers behind your other hand. After the rhyme make a buzzing sound as the bees fly away.

Published by The Voices Foundation
Copyright © The Voices Foundation

More finger rhymes

Mingledy, mingledy, clap, clap, clap,
How many fingers do I hold up?

This little piggy went to market.
(Wiggle thumb, or big toe)
This little piggy stayed at home.
(Second finger/toe)
This little piggy had roast beef,
(Third finger/toe)
And this little piggy had none.
(Fourth finger/toe)
And this little piggy went wee wee wee
All the way home. *(tickle!)*

Open shut them,
Open shut them,
Give a little clap.
Open shut them,
Open shut them,
Lay them in your lap.

This can be used for gathering the children, or quietening them down.

Tickling

Small children love the feeling of anticipation and suspense that these songs and rhymes bring.

Hokey cokey

TRACK 20

You put your left leg in,
your left leg out,

In, out, in, out, shake it all about.

You do the hokey cokey and
you turn around.

That's what it's all about.

Oh - the hokey cokey cokey.
Oh - the hokey cokey cokey.
Oh - the hokey cokey cokey.

Knees bend, arms stretch,
ra ra ra.

This is a good song to sing while dressing the baby or changing her nappy.

What shall we do with the lazy baby?

TRACK 59

What shall we do with the lazy baby?
What shall we do with the lazy baby?
What shall we do with the lazy baby,
Early in the morning?
(CHORUS) Hooray and up she rises,

Hooray and up she rises,

Hooray and up she rises

Early in the morning.

Tickle her toes and rub her tummy…
CHORUS

These words are sung to the tune of "What shall we do with the drunken sailor?". Make up your own verses and include appropriate actions. For example, when changing the baby's nappy, you might lift the baby into the air as you sing the chorus "Hooray and up she rises".

Tickling rhymes

Round and round the garden, like a teddy bear.
One step, two step and tickly under there.

An old favourite, and one which the baby or child will want you to do again and again… You don't have to use the palm. Try starting on the shoulder.

Criss, cross, line, line, *(draw a cross, then two straight lines on the back)*
Spider crawling up your spine, *(walk your fingers upwards)*
Cool breeze, *(blow on the back of the neck)* tight squeeze, *(hug)*
Now you've got the shivers! *(tickle!)*

Children love this rhyme. Do the actions on the baby's or child's back and they will enjoy the gentle touch.

Mice, mice,
eating up the rice,
Nibble, nibble,
nibble, nibble,
nice, nice, nice.

Pretend your fingers are the mice and they are nibbling at different parts of the body.

Let's eat an apple, *(pretend to eat one hand)*
Let's eat a plum, *(pretend to eat the other)*
Let's blow a raspberry on baby's tum. *(Do it!)*

Up and about

Babies from about six months old, and toddlers, love to be bounced on the knee. Their early humour will develop and they will soon learn to bounce rhythmically. Take the lead from the baby who will very quickly let you know if he wants more.

Horsie, horsie

TRACK 21

Horsie, horsie, don't you stop,
Just let your feet go clippety clop,
Your tail goes swish and your wheels go round,
Giddy up, we're homeward bound.

Sit the baby on your lap, or a small child on your foot, and bounce him along to the pulse of the song. Sing the song at a faster or slower tempo.

Cuckoo, cherry tree

TRACK 8

Cuckoo, cherry tree,
Roll the ball, roll to me.

Cuckoo, cherry tree,
Catch the ball, throw to me.

Cuc - koo,   cher-ry   tree,   Catch the   ball,   throw to   me.
                                   (Roll)   (Roll)

Use a soft ball. Roll the ball for a baby; throw the ball for an older child.

Rat-a-tat-tat

TRACK 46

Rat-a-tat-tat! Who is that?
Teddy in his funny hat.

Rat- a- tat- tat! Who is that? Ted- dy in his fun- ny hat.

Small children love to dress up of course; nothing is more fun than wearing different hats. Build up a supply. Having given out hats to four or five children at a time, sing the song for each child in turn, asking them to show off their hat by standing up and turning around when it's their verse.

Going on a picnic

TRACK 14

Going on a picnic, leaving right away.
If it doesn't rain we'll stay all day.
Have you brought the apple?
(solo) Yes, I've brought the apple.
Going on a picnic on a lovely day.

Going to the seaside, leaving right away.
If it doesn't rain we'll stay all day.
Have you brought the sun cream?
(solo) Yes, I've brought the sun cream.
Going to the seaside on a lovely day.

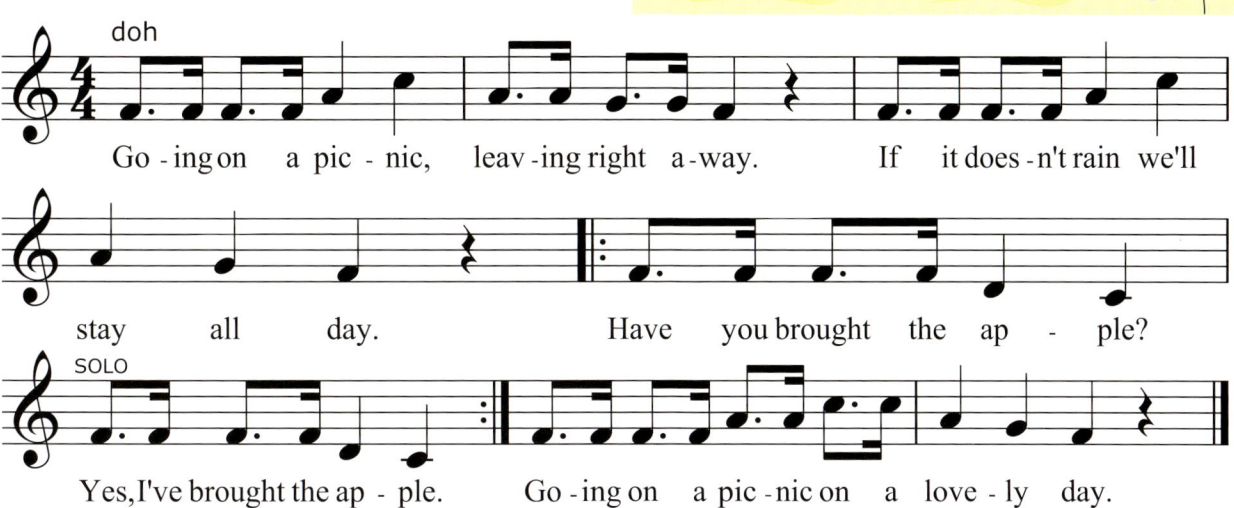

Build up the verses by adding other food to the picnic eg sandwiches, lemonade, biscuits; or other things to the seaside such as t-shirt, sun hat, bucket and spade, so that plenty of children have the chance to sing a solo. Hand out pictures (or real things) to the soloist. Use your own (or the children's) ideas for movements or activities with each verse of the song.

It's raining, it's pouring

TRACK 27

It's raining, it's pouring,
The old man is snoring,
He went to bed and bumped his head
And couldn't get up in the morning.

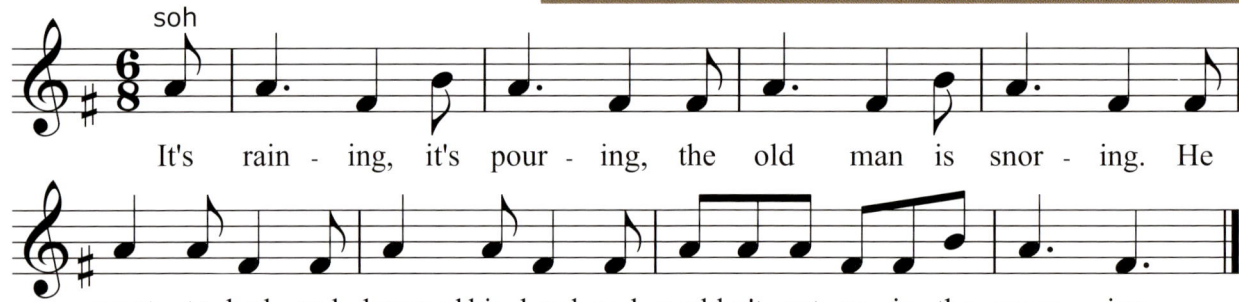

Sway, tap, or clap in time to the pulse as you look out of the window at the miserable weather. Any rain song is also good for bath time or in the water play area. Use your fingers to fall gently like rain drops or fill the watering can and pour out the water.

Published by The Voices Foundation
Copyright © The Voices Foundation

Rain is falling down

TRACK 45

Rain is falling down. (Splash)
Rain is falling down. (Splash)
Pitter patter pitter patter,
Rain is falling down. (Splash)

me

Rain is fal - ling down. (Splash) Rain is fal - ling down. (Splash)

Pit - ter pat - ter pit - ter pat - ter rain is fal - ling down. (Splash)

Whisper each "Splash", with an appropriate action - for example, throwing arms in the air, jumping or clapping.

Up and about

Many rhymes come from the playground. Some chil[dren ... as?]
they say the rhyme. Hold smaller children's hands a[nd ...]
follow the actions.

Chop, chop, chop[...]
Chop off the bott[om ...]
What there is left [...]
Chop, chop, chopp[...]

*Chop the fruit or the [... to]
the pulse of the rhy[me. ...]
fruit salad, or soup, [...]
Put each fruit in an i[maginary bowl in the]
middle of the circle. At [the end of the rhyme]
(when you have added enough!), stir it all
well and taste!*

Handwritten note (24/5/23):
Damian – chose the hand with 5, he matched it to the cake. I asked which number he had he replied 5, showed me 5 fingers, placed 5 candles onto cake & 7.
Raphael same as above. N° 9
Zoe – 10 N°

One, two, three, four,
Mary's at the cottage door.
Five, six, seven, eight,
Eating cherries off a plate.

Jelly on a plate, jelly on a plate.
Wibble wobble, wibble wobble,
Jelly on a plate.

Wiggle your hips like a jelly!

Cat's got the measles, dog's got the flu,
Monkey's got the chickenpox and
So have you!

Published by The Voices Foundation
Copyright © The Voices Foundation

Conversations

It would be a great way to sing conversations with a child. You ask, the child answers. You could sing "Hello, how are you?" to a baby and answer by yourself, "Very well, thank you!" One day the child might answer himself!

For older children, conversation songs and rhymes will help them increase their vocabulary. Understandably, children who don't have English as their first language may be quiet in a nursery situation. Singing songs which are repetitive can be a way for them to surprise you. Of course you can also change the easy call and response songs and sing to the child in her own language.

Hello, how are you?

TRACK 16

Call: Hello, how are you?
Response: Very well, thank you.

Hel - lo, how are you? Ve - ry well, thank you.

This song should be sung informally to small children at the start of the day, as they come into the room perhaps. It might also be used at the beginning of a singing session - which helps the children to understand that the singing time has started. The leader might also select individual children too and add their name - for example, "Hello Lucas, how are you?"

I see you

TRACK 26

Call: I see you.
Response: I see you.
Call: How do you do?
Response: How do you do?

2 Can you run? Yes it is fun.

3 Can you ride? I've never tried.

4 Can you fly? Yes, so goodbye.

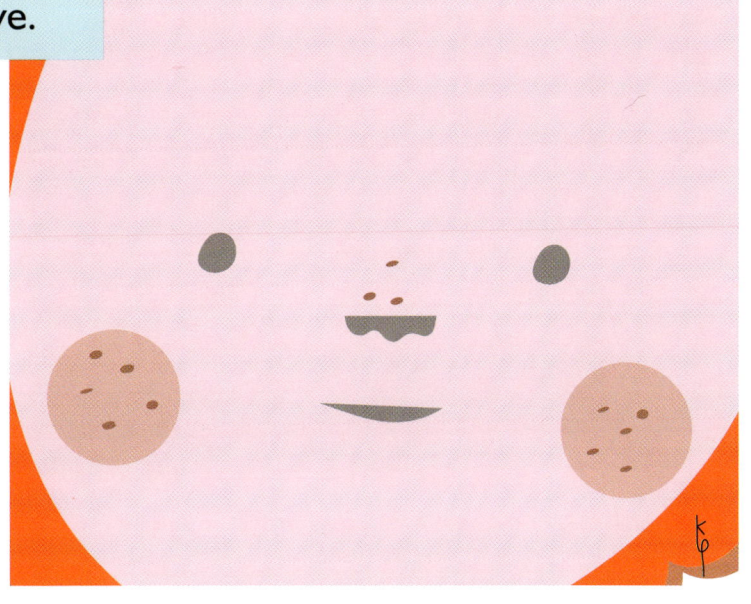

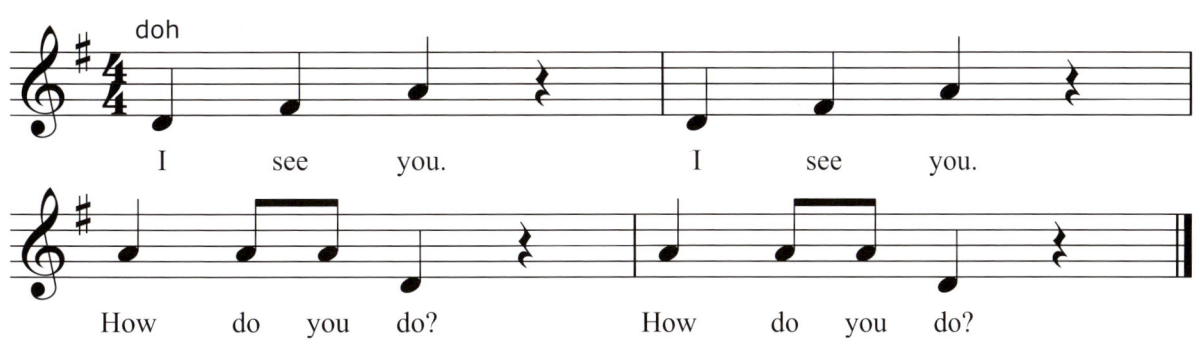

I see you. I see you.
How do you do? How do you do?

This is a useful echo song to help children match your voice. Make up your own verses. Use a puppet with a moveable mouth to sing to the children; they will enjoy singing the response.

Published by The Voices Foundation
Copyright © The Voices Foundation

Charlie over the ocean

TRACK 6

Call: Charlie over the ocean,
Response: Charlie over the ocean.
Call: Charlie over the sea,
Response: Charlie over the sea.
Call: Charlie caught a big fish,
Response: Charlie caught a big fish.
Call: Can't catch me,
Response: Can't catch me.

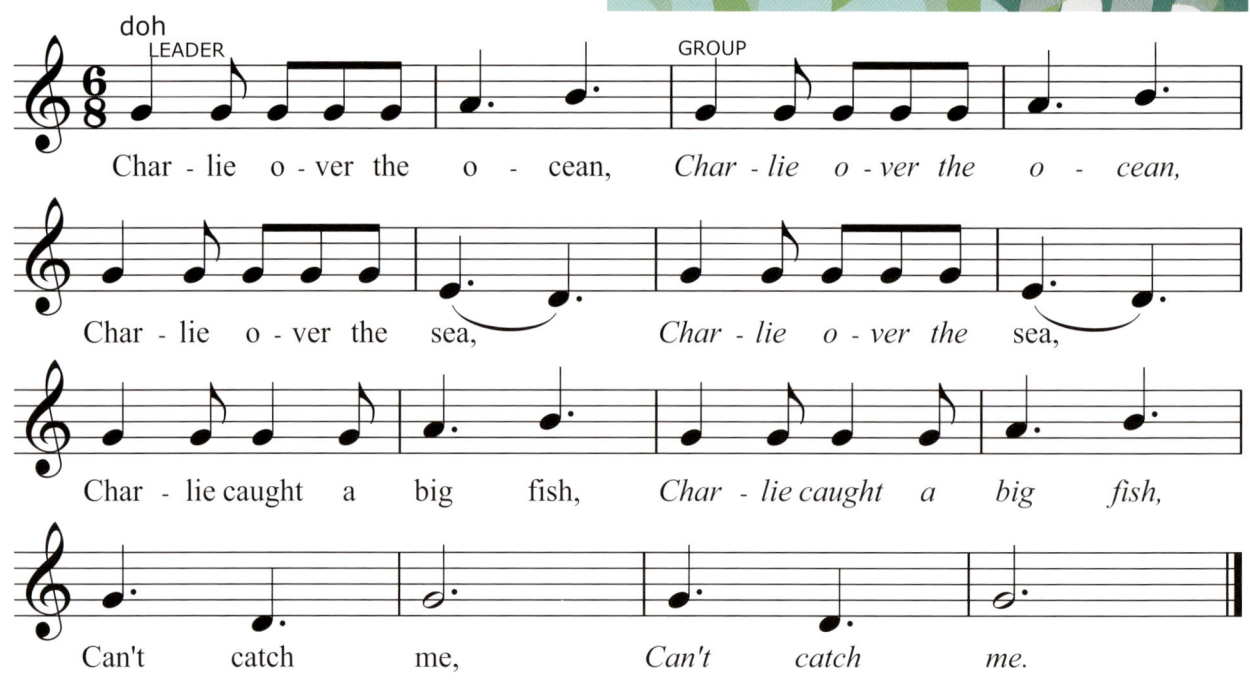

The children form a circle. Carrying a toy fish or a beanbag, the leader walks round the outside of the circle singing the song (Call). Each phrase is echoed by the group (Response). The leader drops the 'fish' behind someone and runs round the circle. The chosen person quickly picks up the 'fish' and runs after the leader, trying to catch her before she reaches the vacant space in the circle.

Doggie, doggie

TRACK 9

All sing:
Doggie, doggie, where's your bone?

Child 1: (dog in the middle):
Someone stole it from my home.

All sing:
Who stole your bone?

Child 2: (someone in the circle):
I stole your bone.

Holding a soft toy to cuddle, Child 1 sits in the middle of a circle, pretending to be the 'doggie'. When his eyes are closed, select Child 2 and give her the 'bone'. At the end of the song, by listening carefully (and not having peeped!), Child 1 recognises the voice of Child 2 and identifies her by name.

Children often have the ability to recognise quickly the timbre of other children's voices - singing as well as speaking.

Conversation rhymes

Cobbler, cobbler mend my shoe,
Have it done by half past two.
Half past two is much too late,
Have it done by half past eight.

This also works as a two note song. Each child can pretend to mend a shoe in time to the pulse. Older children can use rhythm sticks. Divide the group into 2. Half the group can say (or sing) the first two phrases and the others phrases three and four. Then use two confident children to sing or speak by themselves.

Three little birds all fast asleep,
One little bird went, 'Cheep, cheep, cheep.'
Down came Mummy with a big fat crumb
And the first little bird went, 'Yum, yum, yum.'

Two little birds both fast asleep,
One little bird went, 'Cheep, cheep, cheep.'
Down came Mummy with a big fat crumb
And the first little bird went, 'Yum, yum, yum.'

One little bird is fast asleep,
One little bird went, 'Cheep, cheep, cheep.'
Down came Mummy with a big fat crumb
And the first little bird went, 'Yum, yum, yum.'

Follow the actions of the rhyme using three fingers and the other hand. Encourage the children to join in by letting them say 'Cheep, cheep, cheep' and 'Yum, yum, yum' by themselves.

Call and response improvising

Call: Who's got the rabbit?
Response: I've got the rabbit.

Other ideas:
Who's wearing blue today?
I'm wearing blue today.

Who's got long hair?
I've got long hair.

Who has a brother?
I have a brother.

Hand out different toys or finger puppets to the children, asking them to hide them up their jumpers or behind their backs. When the leader sings the question, the toy pops out and the child sings the answer. To avoid confusion, do not distribute too many toys at a time. An alternative is to hand out 3 or 4 of the same puppet to encourage less confident children to respond as a small group, rather than individually.

Curling and stretching

When you sing and move at the same time, children will learn to respond appropriately with large movements. Curl up small and jump up when the music becomes lively, or if the words tell you to. Hide your face with your hands and then shout "boo" on a given cue.

All of this helps to develop spatial awareness too and can be a good start to encourage an active life!

Touch your shoulders

TRACK 56

Touch your shoulders, touch your knees,
Raise your arms and drop them, please,
Touch your ankles, touch your toes,
Pull your ears and touch your nose.

Touch the appropriate parts of the body as you sing the song. Tap each body part twice (but wave your arms for the second phrase). These movements help the children to keep a steady pulse.

Jack in the box

TRACK 28

Jack in the box,
Jack in the box,
Curl down small.
Jack in the box,
Jack in the box,
Jump up tall.

Holding baby in the air, bring her down on to your lap while singing "curl down small"; then lift her back into the air while singing "jump up tall".

Show a toddler how to follow the actions of the song, first curling down, then stretching and jumping up.

Older children first sing the song whilst doing the same actions. Then ask them to sing the song and follow the shape of the melody using hands/arms to show higher and lower.

Teddy bear, teddy bear

TRACK 51

Teddy bear, teddy bear, touch the ground,
Teddy bear, teddy bear, turn right round.
Teddy bear, teddy bear, climb the stairs,
Teddy bear, teddy bear, comb your hair.
Teddy bear, teddy bear, switch off the light,
Teddy bear, teddy bear, say good night.

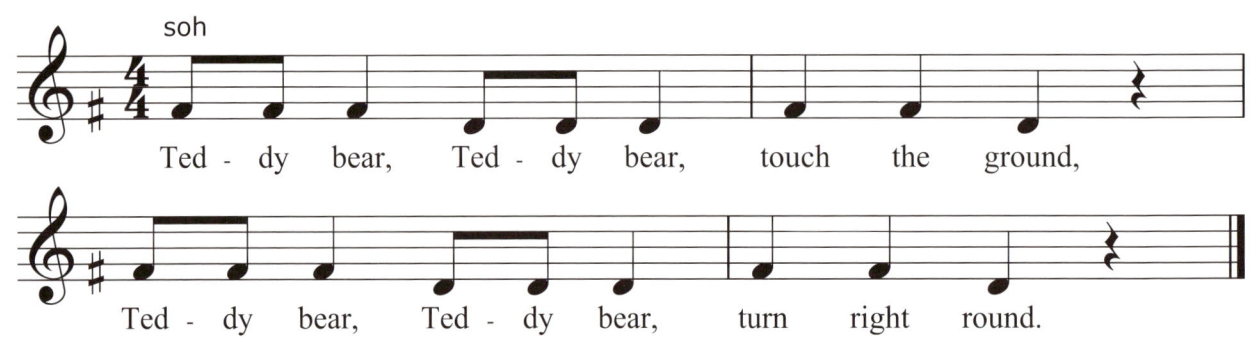

The children can make their favourite bear perform the movements, or they themselves can play the part of a teddy bear.

Published by The Voices Foundation
Copyright © The Voices Foundation

Hey, hey, look at me

TRACK 19

Hey, hey, look at me.
I am jumping*, can you see?
(*clapping, hopping, blinking)

soh

Hey, hey, look at me. I am jump-ing*, can you see?

For toddlers and younger children, sing the song while performing a chosen action; encourage them to echo your singing and copy your actions.

With older children, form a circle and select a confident child to stand in the centre. The child chooses an action and, as you sing, performs the actions in the last two bars; everyone then copies this. A selected older child might be asked to be leader - singing the song and performing his own actions in the last two bars; all the children then repeat this.

N.B. There are only four pulse-actions in each verse (i.e. while singing the last two bars of the song). No actions are performed during the first two bars of the song.

Penny on the water

TRACK 43

Penny on the water, Penny on the sea,
Up jumps a little fish and up jumps ME!

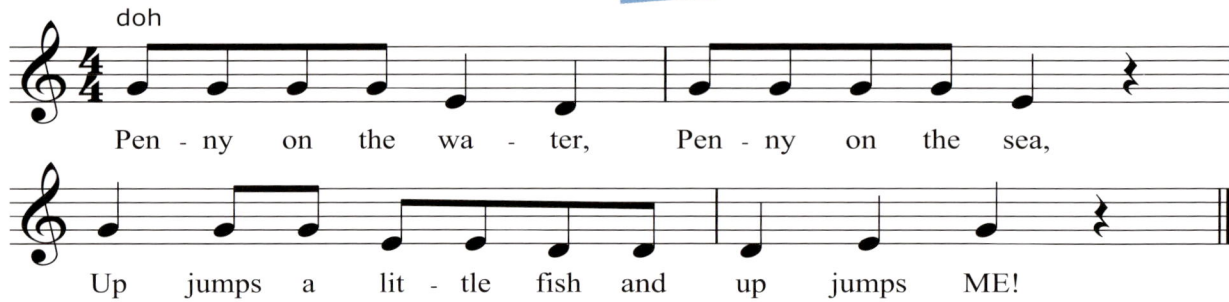

Pen-ny on the wa-ter, Pen-ny on the sea,
Up jumps a lit-tle fish and up jumps ME!

Bounce the baby on your knee. Slow down towards the end of the song, then lift him high on the last word.

Older children might crouch down, jumping up at the end. Alternatively everyone might hold a lycra 'pond' with a toy fish or a beanbag in the middle. Make the fish jump ("jumps") at the beginning of the third phrase and ask the children to jump up ("jumps") at the end of the third phrase.

Curling and stretching rhymes

Up like a rocket, down like the rain,
Back and forwards like a choo choo train.

Zoom zoom zoom, we're going to the moon,
Zoom zoom zoom, we'll be there very soon.
If you want to take a trip,
Climb aboard my rocket ship,
Zoom zoom zoom, we're going to the moon.
5, 4, 3, 2, 1, …. BLAST OFF!

Playing with sounds

Introduce children to language which describes sounds: eg louder and quieter, faster and slower. They will enjoy learning to differentiate between them. Tap out simple repeated rhythms. Children love to use shakers, other instruments and body movement when they hear music.

Different voices

It's a good thing for pre-school children to be able to move fluidly between their different voices:

- Speaking voice
- Singing voice
- Whispering voice. This should be on the breath, not quiet speaking or singing
- Humming voice
- Thinking voice. This is the voice that is inside the head

Children should be encouraged to make clear sounds. Vowel sounds can be disguised as animal noises (baa, neigh, ee-aw, moo). Make up rhymes and jingles emphasising initial sounds of words.

Have you brought your speaking voice?
Answer: Yes I have, yes I have.

Other verses
Have you brought your whispering voice?
Have you brought your humming voice?
Have you brought your thinking voice?
Have you brought your singing voice?

Ask the question using the appropriate voice. The child responds in the same way. 'Thinking voice' means speaking the rhyme in your head. (Make sure that whispering is real, not just quiet speaking or singing). It's up to you if you want to add 'shouting voice'. It is a way of making them realise which one is better for the playground... Shouting should be loud speaking, not loud singing!

Speak/sing appropriate rhymes or songs using various voices.

Use puppets or cue cards to help change the type of voice. For example, as well as speaking, whispering, thinking, (shouting!) - ask the children to use the voice of a princess, a robot, a mouse, or an elephant.

See saw

TRACK 48

See saw, up and down,
In the sky and on the ground.

soh

See - saw, up and down, in the sky and on the ground.

Facing a partner and holding both hands, the children move alternately up and down as if on a see saw.

Published by The Voices Foundation
Copyright © The Voices Foundation

Little bunnies sleeping

TRACK 33

Little bunnies sleeping till it's nearly noon.
Shall we wake them with a merry tune?
Oh so still, are they ill?
Wake up soon!
Hop little bunnies, hop, hop, hop,
Hop hop hop, hop, hop, hop,
Hop little bunnies, hop, hop, hop,
Hop and STOP!

Older children lie 'asleep', very still on the floor. With a gentle, soothing sound, parents/adults sing the first part of the song while the children pretend to be asleep, but are listening.
The more exciting (and faster) second half of the song suddenly begins; the children jump up and hop around the room until they hear "STOP!". (Babies might be gently bounced.)

Published by The Voices Foundation
Copyright © The Voices Foundation

I have sounds

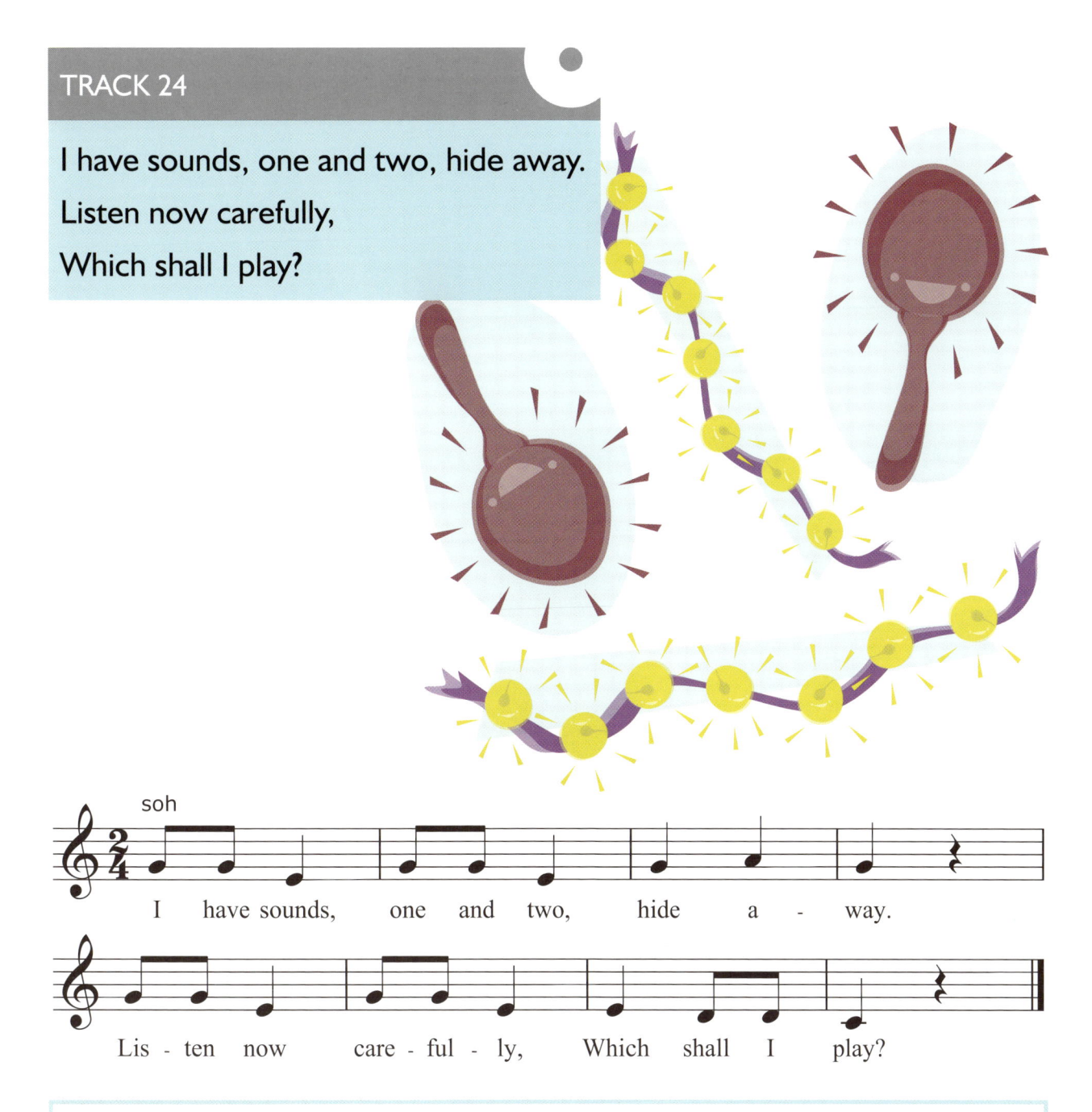

TRACK 24

I have sounds, one and two, hide away.
Listen now carefully,
Which shall I play?

Pick two unpitched percussion instruments and show them to the children, playing each one in turn before hiding them behind your back. Sing the song on your own and then play one of the instruments, unseen behind your back. The children then identify and name the instrument.
Select a child to be the leader. As the children become more confident, choose other unpitched percussion instruments.

The drums in the band

TRACK 52

The drums in the band go boom, boom, boom,

Boom, boom, boom,

Boom, boom, boom,

The drums in the band go boom, boom, boom,

All day long.

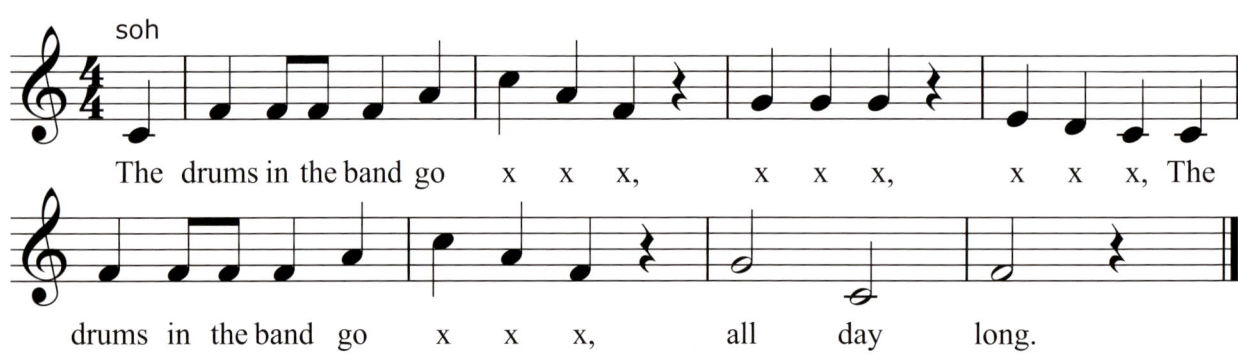

The drums in the band go x x x, x x x, x x x, The drums in the band go x x x, all day long.

Use instruments as indicated by x x x. Change instruments on each verse.

What's in the bag?

TRACK 61

What's in the bag?
What's in the bag?
Can you listen carefully?
What's in the bag?

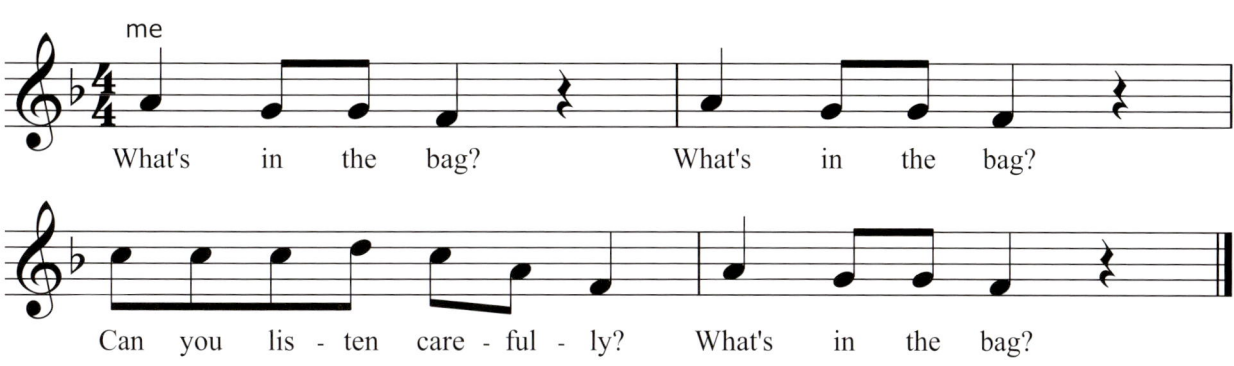

Show the children each instrument, play it and put it in the bag. Then ask each child in turn to feel in the bag, take out an instrument and play it. Or play the instrument inside the bag while the others guess which one is making the sound.

Old MacDonald had a band

TRACK 37

Old MacDonald had a band. EIEIO.
And in that band he had some bells. EIEIO.
With a "ting ting" here and a "ting ting" there,
Here a "ting", there a "ting",
Everywhere a "ting ting",
Old MacDonald had a band. EIEIO.

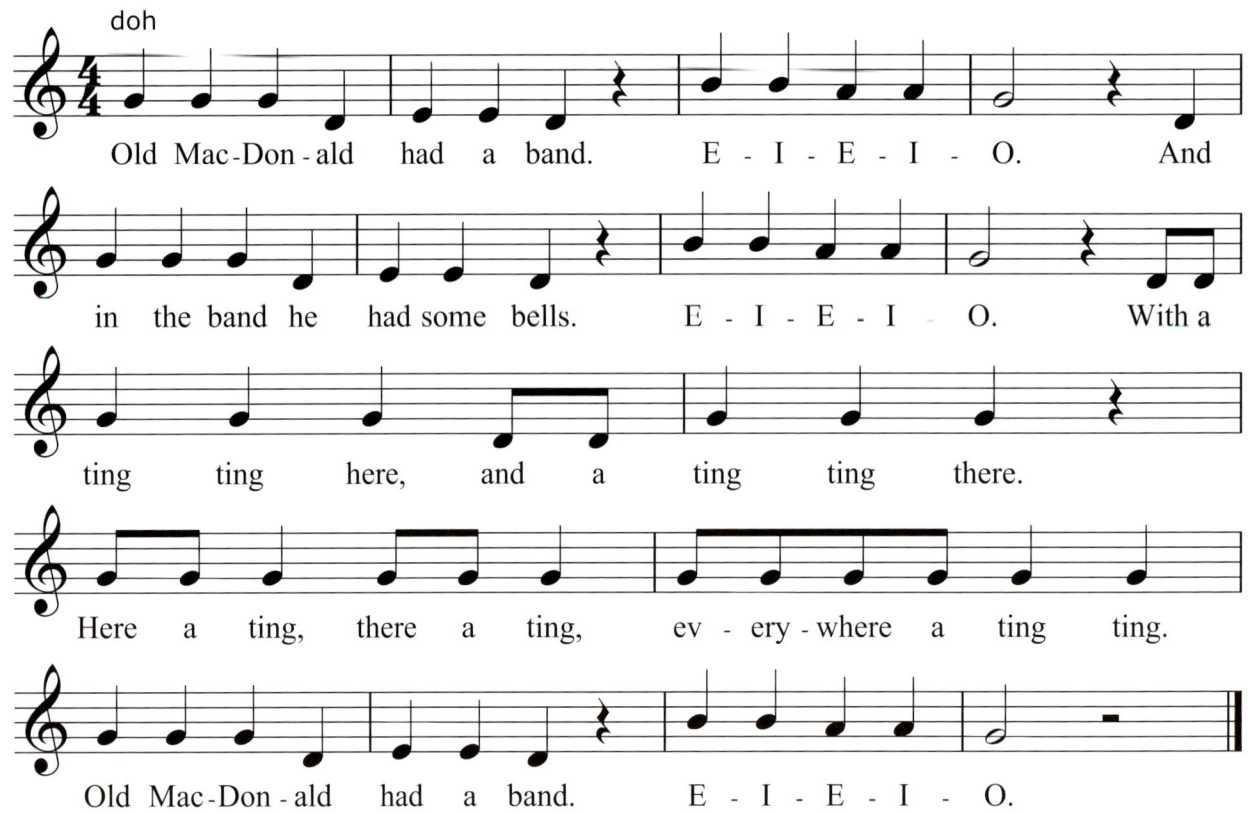

You can change the words:
"… And in that band were things to tap/scrape/shake…"
"…And in that band were wooden/metal/plastic things…"

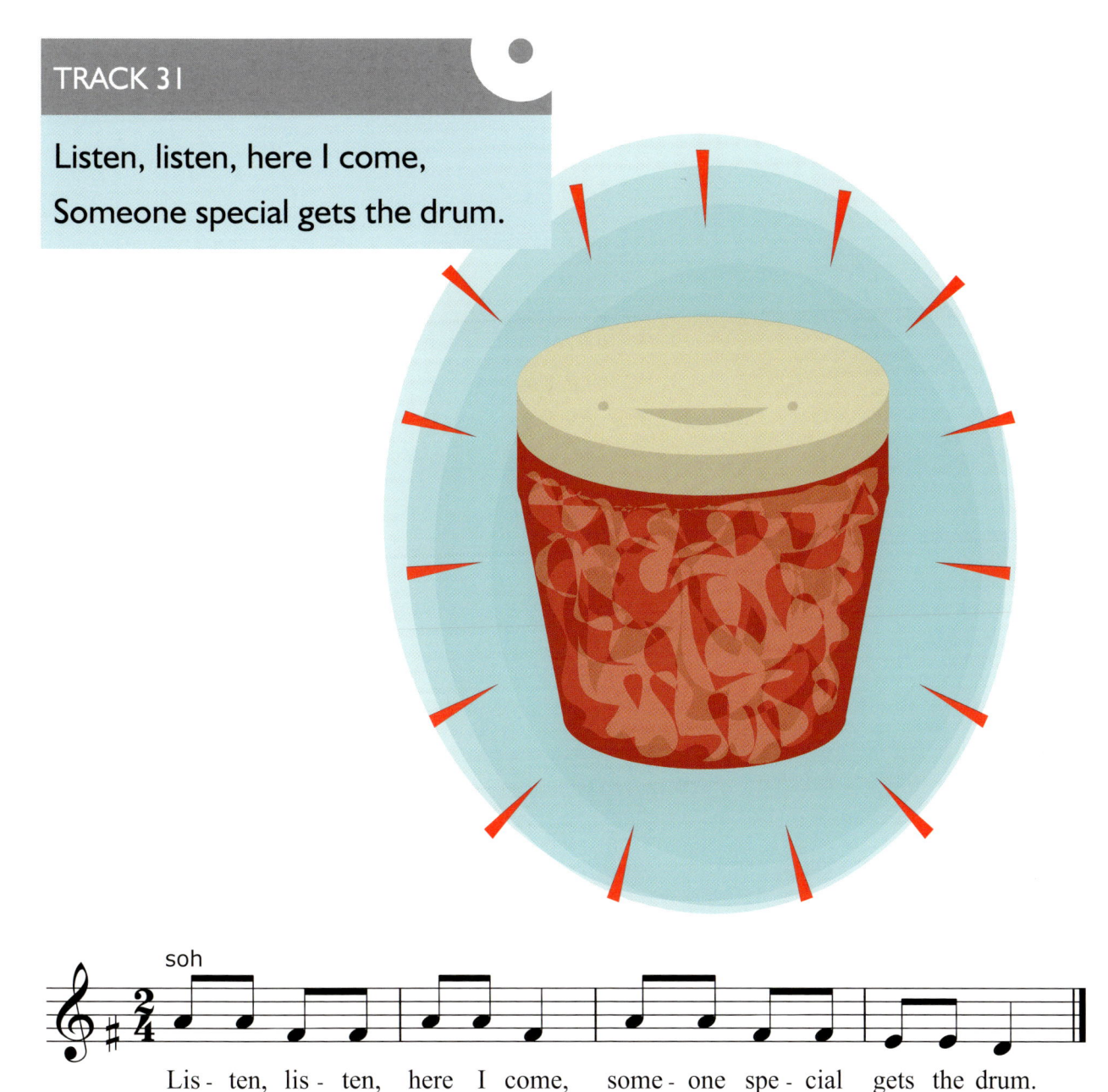

Listen, listen, here I come

TRACK 31

Listen, listen, here I come,
Someone special gets the drum.

Lis-ten, lis-ten, here I come, some-one spe-cial gets the drum.

Form a circle and choose a child to tap the pulse (the heartbeat) or the rhythm (the pattern of the words) on a small drum, as everyone sings the song. Some children may be able to walk round inside the circle and tap at the same time. Others may prefer to stand still. Then the drum is passed to someone else.
Tip: hand the beater to the child first and she will take it with her preferred hand, making it easier to play.

What shall we play in the children's band?

TRACK 60

What shall we play in the children's band,
Children's band, children's band?
What shall we play in the children's band
When we can't go out to play?

We shall play the tambourine…
…the triangle…the big bass drum…

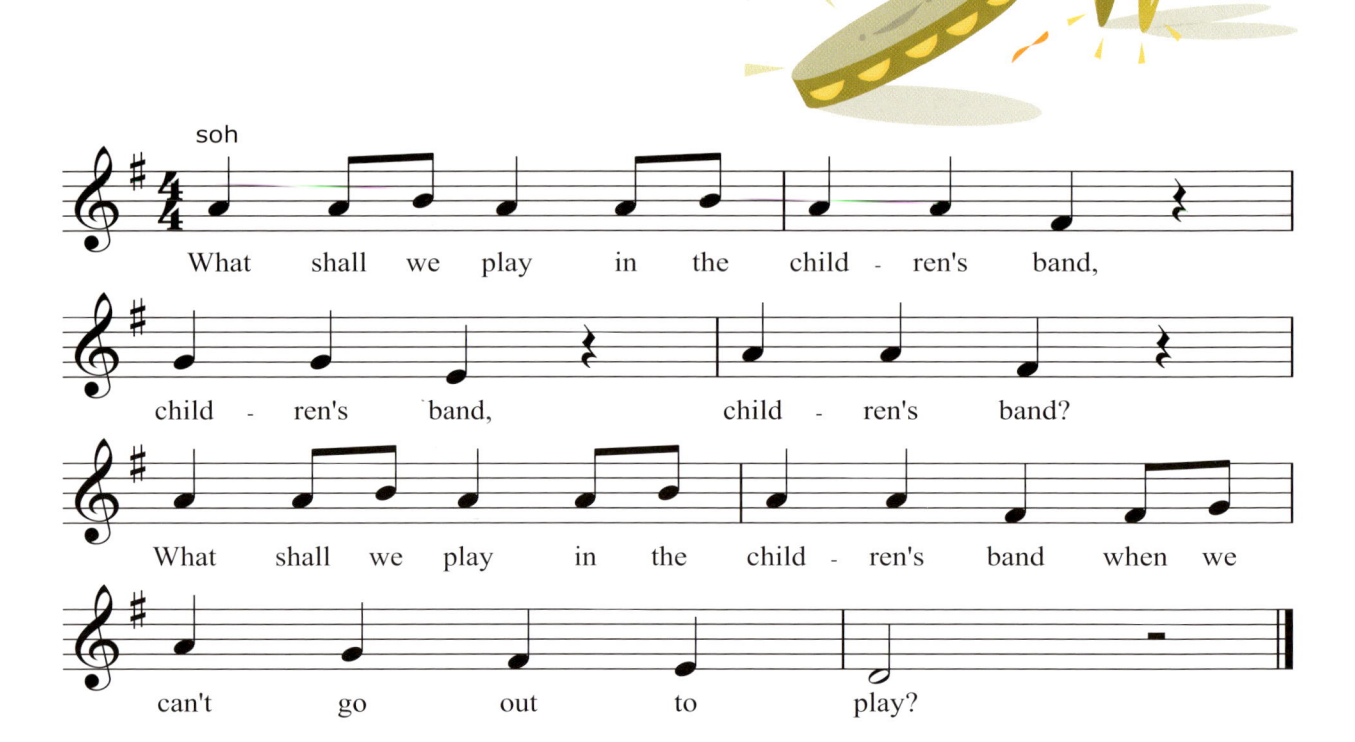

A small group of selected children choose which instrument they would like to play. Name the instruments before playing (and find ways of playing them).

Published by The Voices Foundation
Copyright © The Voices Foundation

Old Mr Woodpecker

TRACK 39

Old Mr Woodpecker sitting in a tree,
Old Mr Woodpecker tapping merrily.

Old Mr Woodpecker you can do it too,
Old Mr Woodpecker this is just for you.

Tap out the rhythm pattern of the song at the end of each phrase. When the children know it well, to make this even more fun, use a puppet to 'sing' the song; but the puppet sings the wrong words for each line. The children will love to put it right. Here are some examples of wrong words: "Old Mr Woodpecker, sitting on my knee… laughing tee hee hee… I'm a kangaroo… Scooby dooby doo".

Signs and symbols

Learning to read starts when children recognise symbols as instructions. Use a mouse puppet (or picture) and a snail to show faster/slower. Make some traffic lights cards for stop, get ready and go. These pictures are the beginning of the journey towards reading. Using puppets is a very positive way of getting the children's attention. They will help the noisy child to settle down, and the quieter one to sing. Leave out the 'props' somewhere and make story boards from the songs you have sung; these will encourage the children to sing by themselves.

Twinkle, twinkle, little star

TRACK 57

Twinkle, twinkle, little star,
How I wonder what you are.
Up above the world so high,
Like a diamond in the sky.
Twinkle, twinkle, little star,
How I wonder what you are.

Remind them that they are using their singing voice and their thinking voice (singing in their head). Use a pop-up puppet to prompt the children when to sing and when not to sing. This will help to focus their attention. They should sing when they can see the puppet and not sing when the puppet hides. It is also a good game to play with groups of children who are shy.

Tick tock, tick tock

TRACK 55

Tick tock, tick tock, see our clock.
Tick tock, tick tock, twelve o'clock.

soh

Tick tock, tick tock, see our clock.
Tick tock, tick tock, twelve o' clock.

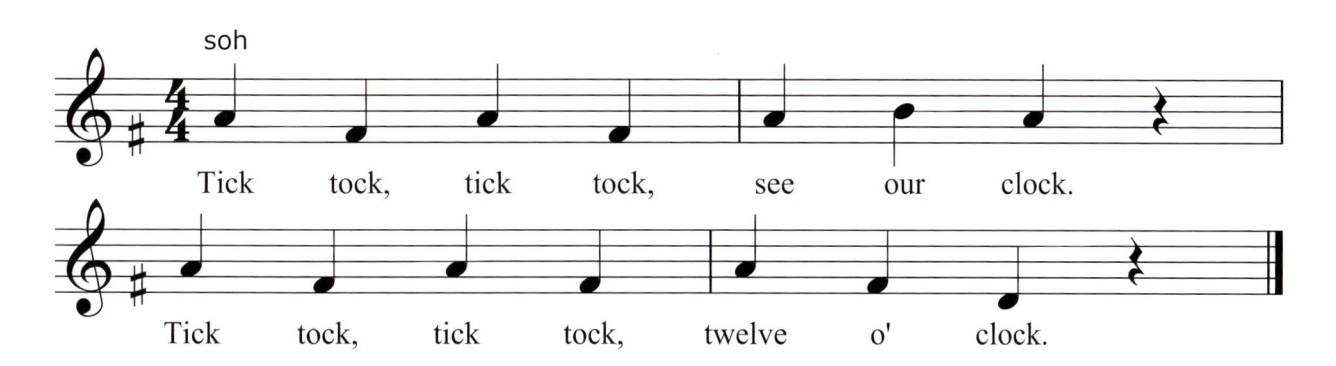

Change the time on your play clock and count the numbers with the children until you reach the correct o'clock. Then sing the song together.

On a log

TRACK 40

On a log, Mr Frog
Sang his song the whole day long.
Glumf, glumf, glumf, glumf.

On a log, Mis-ter Frog sang his song the whole day long. Glumf, glumf, glumf, glumf.

A selected child plays the part of Mr (or Mrs) Frog and crouches in the centre of the circle, ready to jump like a frog on the last four words. Alternatively use the lycra 'pond' with a toy frog. Keep it very still until the end when the frog jumps on the four beats. Try introducing some notation by showing the rhythm of the glumfs as four large frogs (crotchets). These could be substituted with eight little frogs (quavers). Very clever children might read a combination of crotchets and quavers and sing the "glumfs" accordingly.

Circle games

Taking part in circle games is something everyone will remember from their own early childhood. It is a rite of passage!

Learning the complex structures of verses ("The farmer's in his den") or actions ("Here we go round the mulberry bush") is an important step towards numeracy.

Performing movements correctly requires good motor skills and spatial awareness.

The 'game elements' of these activities are enjoyed by the children. But they also contribute significantly to the children's social skills such as 'taking turns' and 'choosing partners'.

Sally go round the sun

TRACK 47

Sally go round the sun,
Sally go round the moon,
Sally go round the chimney pots
Ev'ry afternoon. JUMP!

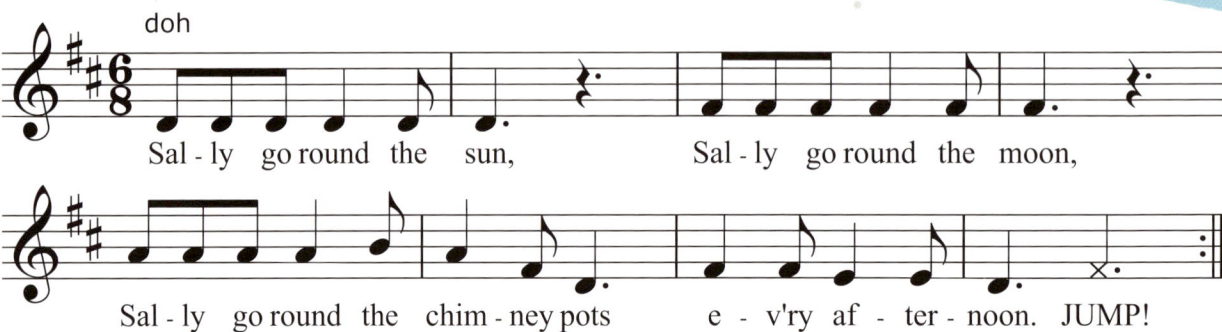

The children walk round in a circle keeping the pulse with their feet and singing the song. Ask them to use their shouting voice on every "JUMP!". Sing the song several times and, as children grow in confidence change the walking direction and the type of voice for each "JUMP!" (eg whispering, speaking, etc). End with the 'thinking voice' so that the children will feel the pulse clearly. Alternatively, ask the children to lie on the floor under a parachute while the adults in the group walk in a circle, holding it just above their heads. They will love this!

Published by The Voices Foundation
Copyright © The Voices Foundation

Here sits a mousie

TRACK 17

Here sits a mousie
(make the whiskers with your fingers)
In his little housie.
(join hands over your head in the shape of a house)
No-one comes to see him,
(hands out palms up)
Poor little mousie.
(make crying patterns down your cheeks)

Mousie chooses a person and sings Have you got my bells?
And the response can be
Yes I have, yes I have (or no I haven't, no I haven't!)

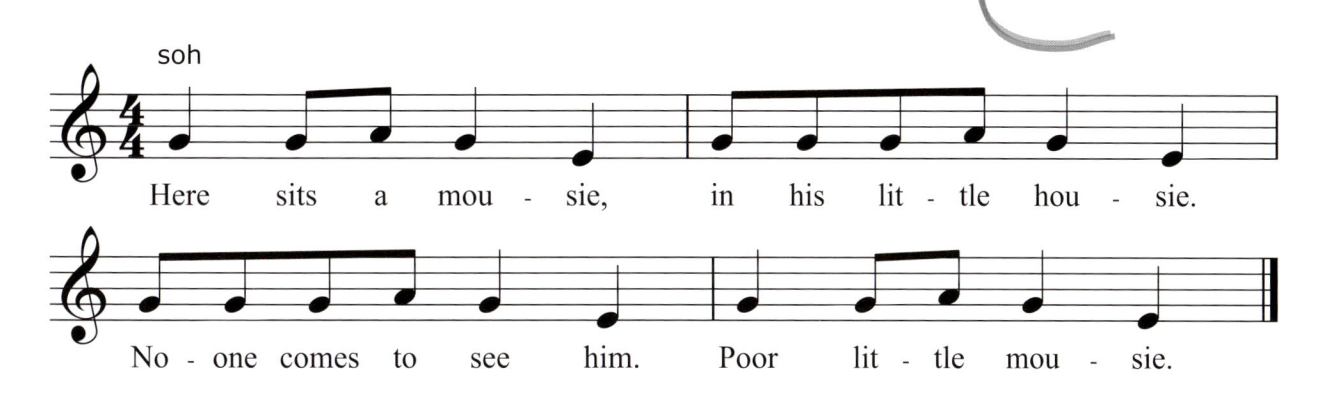

soh

Here sits a mou-sie, in his lit-tle hou-sie.
No-one comes to see him. Poor lit-tle mou-sie.

'Mousie' sits in the middle of a circle, with a stick of bells on the floor behind him. While singing the song, the group performs four identical actions to the four beats of each bar, changing the actions in successive bars. At the end of the song, a selected child quietly 'steals' the bells from behind 'Mousie' (no peeping!) and hides them. Having heard some noise from the bells, 'Mousie' (hopefully) will have some idea where they might be and indicates where he thinks they are. Occasionally, a little help might be required.

Early in the morning

TRACK 11

Early in the morning at eight o'clock,
You can hear the postman knock.
Up jumps John, to open the door,
One letter, two letters, three letters, four.

Sit or stand in a circle. The postman (or woman!) walks around until the words "postman knock", when he stops in front of someone and taps on their shoulder. Up jumps the child and pretends to open the door. The postman then 'delivers' four letters as the four numbers are sung. The other children might clap along too.

Can you dance?

TRACK 5

Can you dance Santa Maloney?
Can you dance Santa Maloney?
Can you dance Santa Maloney
And turn yourself about?

Place your hand on your shoulder (x3) and turn yourself about.

Place your hand on your left hand.......etc

Can you dance San-ta Ma-lo-ney? Can you dance San-ta Ma-lo-ney? Can you dance San-ta Ma-lo-ney and turn your-self a-bout?

Make up a movement for the chorus and follow the words in the verses. Add your own actions too.

Here comes a bluebird

TRACK 18

Here comes a bluebird through the window,
Hey diddle-dum-a day day day.
Take a little partner, hop in the garden,
Hey diddle-dum-a day day day.

soh

Here comes a blue-bird through the ___ win-dow, hey did-dle-dum-a day day day. Take a lit-tle part-ner, hop in the gar-den, hey did-dle-dum-a day day day.

Make a circle with the children holding their hands high to make 'windows'. The chosen bluebird walks or runs in and out of the 'windows' until she takes a little partner. They then hop or dance in the circle until the end of the song. Then the first child joins the circle and the second child becomes the bluebird.

Published by The Voices Foundation
Copyright © The Voices Foundation

Old King Glory

TRACK 36

Old King Glory on the mountain,

The mountain was so high that it nearly touched the sky,

And it's one, two, three, follow me.

Last phrase of last verse…
And we all bow down to the mountain.

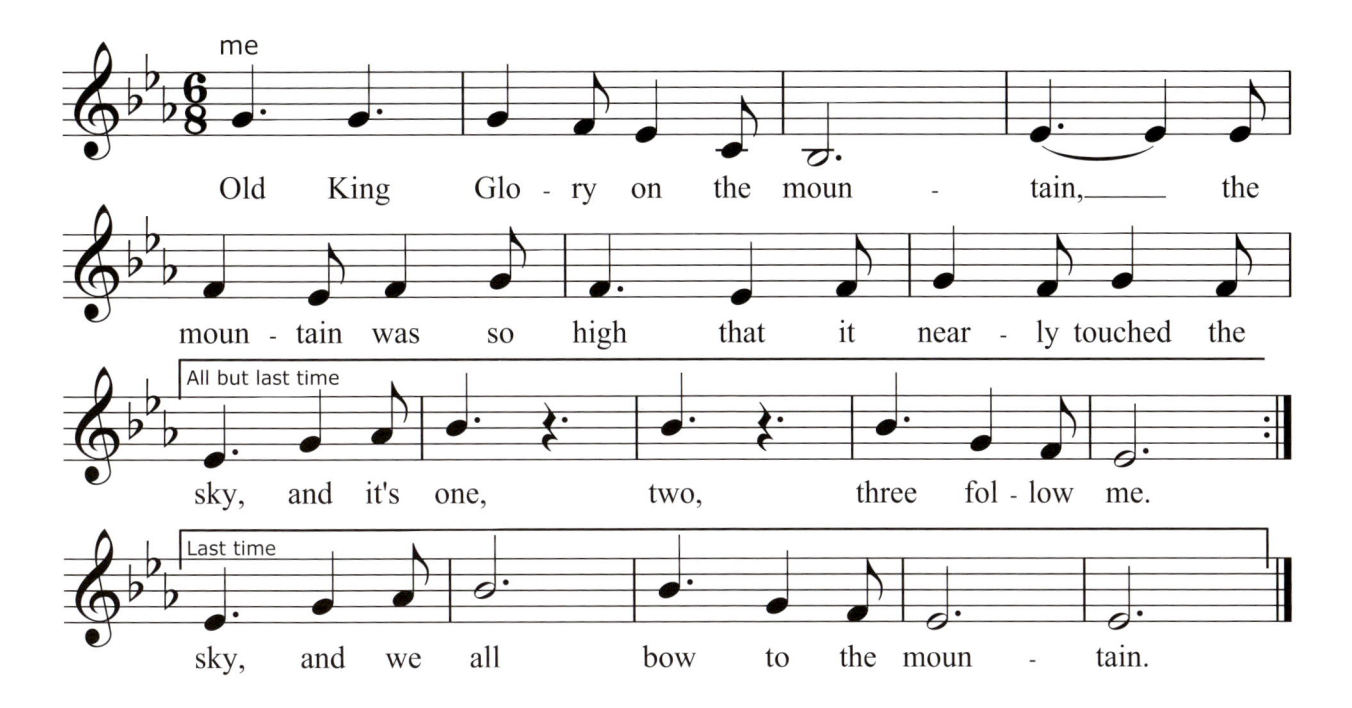

Old King Glo-ry on the moun-tain,___ the moun-tain was so high that it near-ly touched the

All but last time
sky, and it's one, two, three fol-low me.

Last time
sky, and we all bow to the moun-tain.

The children form a circle, and the leader stands outside it. The children walk round one way during the song while the leader (often a grown up) walks round the other way. On the words "one, two, three follow me", the leader taps three children on the shoulder as she passes. These children then leave the inside circle and join the outside one. A second verse is sung, with three more children being chosen. When there are fewer than three people left in the inner circle, all sing the last verse and the remainder become the next leaders. (With a small group, you could choose only one person to follow the leader each time.)

Published by The Voices Foundation
Copyright © The Voices Foundation

Witch, witch, fell in a ditch

TRACK 64

Witch, witch, fell in a ditch,
Picked up a penny and thought she was rich.
(Witch sings) Are you my children?
(All) Yes, we're your children.
(Witch sings) Are you my children?
(All) Yes, we're your children.
(Witch sings) Are you my children?
(All say) NO WE'RE NOT!

The children form a circle facing outwards. The 'witch' stands in the middle. She picks up the penny then drops it behind someone who becomes the next 'witch'. The children turn round on "NO WE'RE NOT!".

Jump, jump, jump Jim Joe

TRACK 29

Jump, jump, jump Jim Joe,

Shake your head and nod your head and tap your toe.

Round, round, round you go,

Then you choose another partner

And you jump Jim Joe.

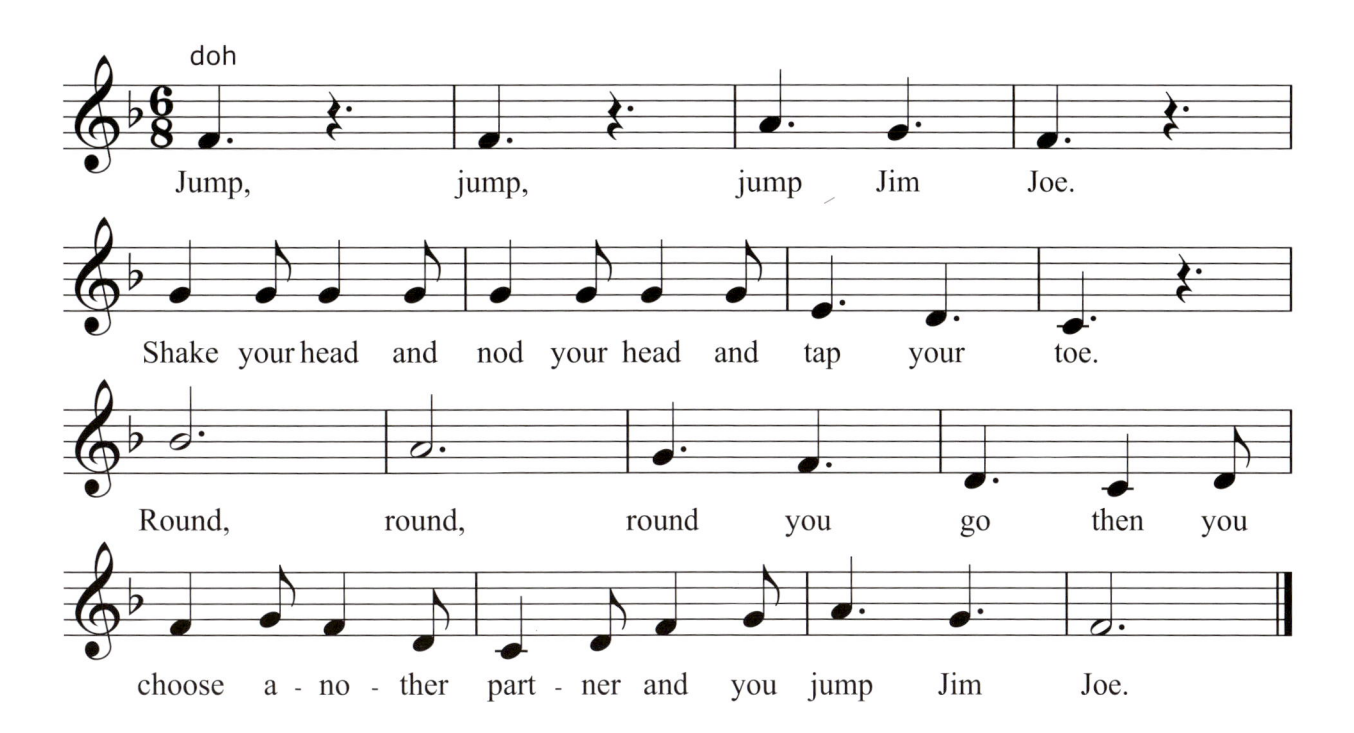

The actions follow the words of the song. There are different ways to organise this.
1. Start with two children, each of whom chooses another partner, making 4, then 8, then 16, then everyone!
2. Use only two or three pairs.
Knowing how to stop can become an issue because the children really love jumping and changing partners. You could sing "you stop Jim Joe" or "it's time to go".

Published by The Voices Foundation
Copyright © The Voices Foundation

Down came Andrew

TRACK 10

Down came (Andrew), down came he.
He is hiding the button and the key.
Who has the button?
(Child answers) I have the button.
Who has the key?
(Child answers) I have the key.

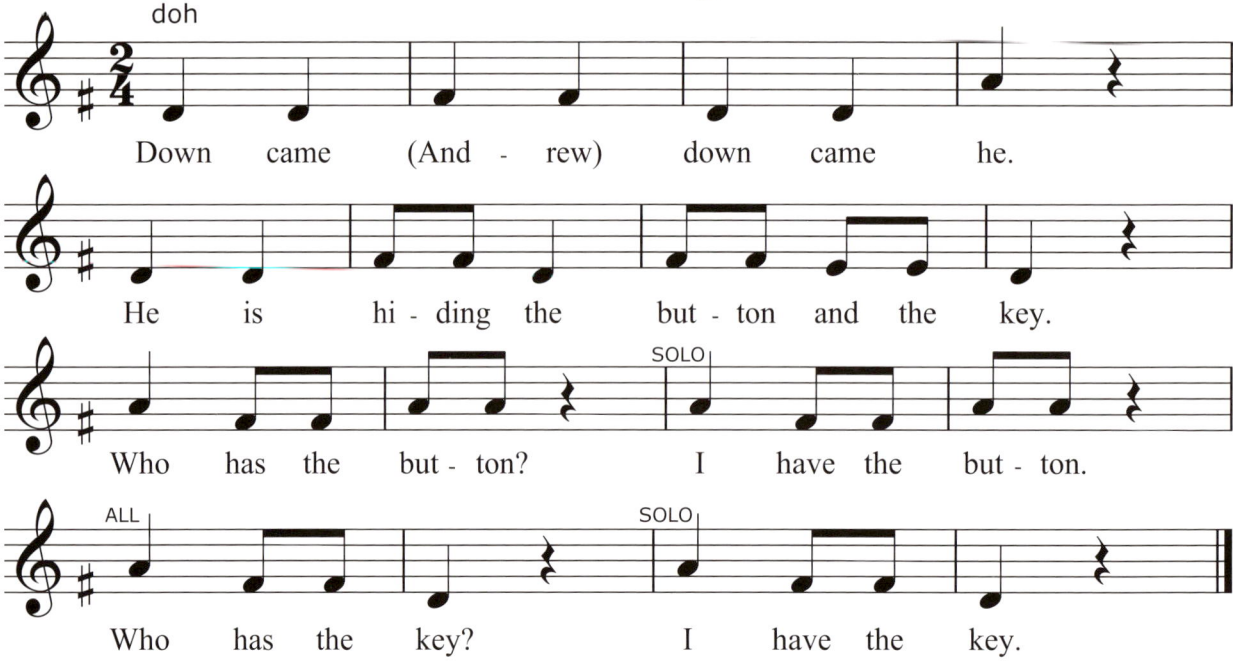

Down came (And-rew) down came he.
He is hi-ding the but-ton and the key.
Who has the but-ton? **SOLO** I have the but-ton.
ALL Who has the key? **SOLO** I have the key.

Form a circle with a selected child in the middle, covering her eyes with her hands. Then allocate the button to one child in the circle and the key to another. (Choose confident children at the start of the game.) As the song is sung, the button and key holders sing on their own (as shown). The child in the middle of the ring listens carefully to the solo voices and identifies who has the button and who has the key.

Published by The Voices Foundation
Copyright © The Voices Foundation

Listening material

The listening material on the accompanying CD has been carefully chosen to correspond to the activity topics. Details are provided on the following pages.

WIEGENLIED (CRADLE SONG) — TRACK 66

Composer	Franz Schubert
Performers	Christoph Genz (tenor) and Wolfram Rieger (piano)
Time	2.07 minutes
Source	Naxos 8.554790

Composed as a cradle song. Rock a young child to and fro as you both listen to the music.

LULLABY, Op. 49, No.4 — TRACK 67

Composer	Johannes Brahms
Performer	Idil Biret (piano)
Time	2.11 minutes
Source	Naxos 8.554790

Composed as a cradle song. Rock a young child to and fro as you both listen to the music.

TEDDY BEARS' PICNIC — TRACK 68

Composer	John Bratton
Performer	Billy Costello
Time	3.31 minutes
Source	Naxos 8.120704

As the recording is played, make a teddy bear or other soft toy dance in front of the baby. Ask older children to make their own teddy dance and take it along to an imaginary picnic.

DANCE OF THE SUGAR-PLUM FAIRY (THE NUTCRACKER, Op. 71a) — TRACK 69

Composer	Peter Illich Tchaikovsky
Performer	Slovak PO conducted by Michael Halasz
Time	1.48 minutes
Source	Naxos 8.550050

Play with a baby's fingers and toes in time to the music. Suggest that older children dance on tiptoes and move their arms, hands and fingers expressively.

THE TYPEWRITER — TRACK 70

Composer	Leroy Anderson
Performer	Richard Hayman and His Orchestra
Time	1.50 minutes
Source	Naxos 8.559125

Face the baby and tickle tummy, hands and feet in time to the music.
When you begin to know the music well, you will be able to anticipate where little pauses and slowing ups come in the music and express this in your movements.

PIZZICATO POLKA — TRACK 71

Composer	Johann Strauss II
Performer	Slovak State PO, Kosice conducted by Alfred Walter
Time	2.57 minutes
Source	Naxos 8.555811

As with Track 70, face the baby and tickle tummy, hands and feet in time to the music.
When you begin to know the music well, you will be able to anticipate where little pauses and slowing ups come in the music and express this in your movements.

THE ENTRY OF THE GLADIATORS Op. 68 (TRIUMPH MARCH) — TRACK 72

Composer	Julius Fucik
Performer	Royal Swedish Airforce Band conducted by Jerher Johanssen
Time	2.59 minutes
Source	Naxos 8.557545

This music is associated with circus parades. Help very young children to walk around the room like a big parade while others wave and clap. Older children might imitate clowns, jugglers and other circus performers.

PARADE OF THE TIN SOLDIERS — TRACK 73

Composer	Leon Jessel
Performer	Balasz Szokolay (piano)
Time	2.51 minutes
Source	Naxos 8.555812

Carry babies around, stepping in time to the music. Invite older children to march like toy soldiers.

HORSE AND BUGGY — TRACK 74

Composer	Leroy Anderson
Performer	BBC Concert Orchestra, conducted by Leonard Slatkin
Time	3.46 minutes
Source	Naxos 8.559356

Bounce young children on your knee as though they are riding in the buggy. Perhaps they can pretend to hold the reins.
Invite older children to move round the room like the horse. Can they hear the sounds of the horses hooves and the crack of the driver's whip? The middle section becomes slower as the horse gets tired, but then trots home speedily at the end. Discuss faster and slower with the older children.

Published by The Voices Foundation
Copyright © The Voices Foundation

RUSSIAN DANCE (THE NUTCRACKER, Op. 71a) — TRACK 75

Composer	Peter Illich Tchaikovsky
Performer	Slovak PO conducted by Michael Halasz
Time	1.11 minutes
Source	Naxos 8.550050

This is the dance of the Cossacks in Tchaikovsky's ballet. As they dance they curl down and stretch up with hands in the air. At the beginning we can imagine them doing this. In other sections of the music we hear them spinning around very fast.

UYAMEMZA — TRACK 76

Composer	Traditional African Song arranged by Eeor Koivistoinen
Performer	Alexandra Youth Choir
Time	2.45 minutes
Source	Naxos 76025-2

This is a conversation between a small group of women who sing out to their friends; then their friends reply (call and response). It is a conversation through singing. Having listened to it, suggest that a child copies this idea by making up a singing call and have a friend respond. Do children know any other call and response songs?

THE WALTZING CAT — TRACK 77

Composer	Leroy Anderson
Performer	Richard Hayman and His Orchestra
Time	2.57 minutes
Source	Naxos 8.559125

This music is played by stringed instruments. The sounds of the cat miaowing are heard as it waltzes. Ask the children to move like a cat and pretend to miaow with the cat.

PLINK, PLANK, PLUNK — TRACK 78

Composer	Leroy Anderson
Performer	Richard Hayman and His Orchestra
Time	2.55 minutes
Source	Naxos 8.559125

This cheerful little piece contains a variety of percussion sounds played by many different instruments including hooters, woodblocks etc. Ask the children if your class music table has any of the instruments they hear in the music. Invite them to 'accompany' the piece with a chosen percussion instrument.

Published by The Voices Foundation
Copyright © The Voices Foundation

MUSETTE (ANNA MAGDALENA'S NOTEBOOK) — TRACK 79

Composer	Johann Sebastian Bach
Performer	Janos Sebestyen (piano)
Time	0.54 minutes
Source	Naxos 8.557579-80

This piece has three very short sections. The first and third sections are the same. In the first and third sections the melody moves from higher to lower and back again. Can the children show higher and lower by moving their arms up and down as they hear the melody move from higher to lower? In the middle section they should listen quietly until the third section begins.

INCHWORM — TRACK 80

Composer	Frank Loesser
Performer	Danny Kaye
Time	3.17 minutes
Source	Naxos 8.120775

This is a counting and measuring song. Also it is a song about mini-beasts! Can the children hear the numbers in the song as the Inchworm measures?

CAN-CAN (ORPHEUS IN THE UNDERWORLD) — TRACK 81

Composer	Jacques Offenbach
Performer	Slovak State PO conducted by Johannes Wildner
Time	2.13 minutes
Source	Naxos 8.555811

The music of the Can-Can makes us want to move and to dance. Can the children move round and round in a circle as they dance? Don't get dizzy!!

LARGO FROM OBOE CONCERTO IN G MINOR — TRACK 82

Composer	Johann Sebastian Bach
Performer	Christian Hommel (oboe) and Cologne Chamber Orchestra conducted by Helmut Muller-Bruhl
Time	2.52 minutes
Source	Naxos 8.557579-80

This is a slower piece of music. Arrange for the children to hold floaty silk scarves or ribbons and to make circle patterns in the air and on the ground as they move their arms in time to the music. Make bubbles to float in the air for younger children to watch as the music is played. Moving slowly, in time to the music, the children make circle patterns in the sand tray or draw circles on paper with crayons and markers. Ask what colours they will use? How has the music suggested these colours?

Published by The Voices Foundation
Copyright © The Voices Foundation

Index of songs and rhymes by activity

Rocking (Page 9)
Bye Baby Bunting
Sleep, baby, sleep
Suogân
Lullaby my baby
Hari coo coo
Ally bally bee
Allundé

Looking and listening (Page 17)
Hush little baby
You are my sunshine
Over in the meadow
Lavender's blue
Pitter, patter
What shall we do?

Joining in (Page 25)
Five little monkeys
Old MacDonald had a farm
Pease pudding hot
There's a spider on my toe
The little green frog
Incey Wincey spider
Clap, clap, clap your hands
Ickle ockle, blue bottle
Easter eggs
Little baby, fast asleep
Where, oh where are all the babies?
Where is Georgie?
Joining-in rhymes

Finding those fingers and toes (Page 41)
Magic fingers
All the little ducks
Finger rhymes
More finger rhymes

Tickling (Page 47)
Hokey cokey
What shall we do with the lazy baby?
Tickling rhymes

Up and about (Page 51)
Horsie, horsie
Cuckoo, cherry tree
Rat-a-tat-tat
Going on a picnic
It's raining, it's pouring
Rain is falling down
'Up and about' rhymes

Conversations (Page 59)
Hello, how are you?
I see you
Charlie over the ocean
Doggie, doggie
Conversation rhymes
Call and response improvising

Curling and stretching (Page 67)
Touch your shoulders
Jack-in-the-box
Teddy bear, teddy bear
Hey, hey, look at me
Penny on the water
Curling and stretching rhymes

Playing with sounds (Page 75)
Different voices
See saw
Little bunnies sleeping
I have sounds
The drums in the band
What's in the bag?
Old MacDonald had a band
Listen. listen, here I come
What shall we play?
Old Mr Woodpecker

Signs and symbols (Page 87)
Twinkle, twinkle, little star
Tick tock, tick tock
On a log

Circle games (Page 91)
Sally go round the sun
Here sits a mousie
Early in the morning
Can you dance?
Here comes a bluebird
Old King Glory
Witch, witch, fell in a ditch
Jump, jump, jump Jim Joe
Down came Andrew

Published by The Voices Foundation
Copyright © The Voices Foundation

Alphabetical index of rhymes and chants

	Page		Page
Apples, peaches, pears and plums	40	Mice, mice	50
Cat's got the measles	58	Mingledy, mingledy	46
Chop, chop, choppety chop	58	Mum and Dad and Uncle John	39
Cobbler, cobbler mend my shoe	64	One potato, two potato	44
Criss, cross, line, line	50	One, two, three, four	58
Fingers like to wiggle waggle	44	Open shut them	46
Five fat sausages	38	Roly poly roly poly	44
Five little peas in a pea pod pressed	45	Round and round the garden	50
Ha ha ha, hee hee hee	40	Swing me over the ocean	39
Here are grandma's glasses	38	This little piggy went to market	46
Here is the beehive	45	Three little birds	64
Jelly on a plate, jelly on a plate	58	Two little dickie birds sitting on a wall	44
Johnny Johnny	45	Up like a rocket	73
Let's eat an apple	50	Zoom zoom zoom	73

Published by The Voices Foundation
Copyright © The Voices Foundation

Alphabetical index of songs

Song Title	Page	Track
All the little ducks	43	1
Allundé	16	2
Ally bally bee	15	3
Bye baby bunting	10	4
Can you dance?	95	5
Charlie over the ocean	62	6
Clap, clap, clap your hands	32	7
Cuckoo, cherry tree	53	8
Doggie, doggie	63	9
Down came Andrew	100	10
Early in the morning	94	11
Easter eggs	34	12
Five little monkeys	26	13
Going on a picnic	55	14
Hari coo coo	14	15
Hello, how are you?	60	16
Here comes a bluebird	96	17
Here sits a mousie	93	18
Hey, hey, look at me	71	19
Hokey cokey	48	20
Horsie, horsie	52	21
Hush little baby	18	22
I have sounds	79	23
I see you	61	24
Ickle ockle, blue bottle	33	25
Incey Wincey spider	31	26
It's raining, it's pouring	56	27
Jack in the box	69	28
Jump, jump, jump Jim Joe	99	29
Lavender's blue	21	30
Listen, listen, here I come	83	31
Little baby, fast asleep	35	32
Little bunnies sleeping	78	33
Lullaby my baby	13	34

Song Title	Page	Track
Magic fingers	42	35
Old King Glory	97	36
Old MacDonald had a band	82	37
Old MacDonald had a farm	27	38
Old Mr Woodpecker	85	39
On a log	90	40
Over in the meadow	20	41
Pease pudding hot	28	42
Penny on the water	72	43
Pitter patter	22	44
Rain is falling down	57	45
Rat-a-tat-tat	54	46
Sally go round the sun	92	47
See saw	77	48
Sleep baby sleep	11	49
Suogân	12	50
Teddy bear, teddy bear	70	51
The drums in the band	80	52
The little green frog	30	53
There's a spider on my toe	29	54
Tick tock, tick tock	89	55
Touch your shoulders	68	56
Twinkle, twinkle, little star	88	57
What shall we do with the lazy baby?	49	58
What shall we do when the baby cries?	23	59
What shall we play in the children's band?	84	60
What's in the bag?	81	61
Where is Georgie?	37	62
Where, oh where are all the babies?	36	63
Witch, witch, fell in a ditch	98	64
You are my sunshine	19	65

Published by The Voices Foundation
Copyright © The Voices Foundation

Skills and concepts

Musical skills are subconscious at first. For example, we don't tell tiny children to march to the beat. At some point decisions can be made about when to introduce these skills. When working with children from 0-5 the most important singing step is to build up their repertoire. Sing songs with them every day; the children gradually will begin to join in and really enjoy the sound of voices. When the children seem ready, teachers can begin to make musical skills and concepts conscious to them. Below is a list of musical skills.

Different voices

There are lots of different voices in our heads. Sing songs in singing voices, say rhymes in talking voices; then change to whispering (which is on the breath, not quiet singing), humming and thinking. Shouting is an option!! You can add others too eg higher and lower, grumpy, happy voices.

Rhythm

This follows the pattern of the words. Use two fingers and tap onto the other hand. When this is established, use the thinking voice and invite the children to let their fingers sing the song! Add two or three instruments like rhythm sticks or claves. Use simple, tight tapped sounds for rhythm work rather than shaking instruments which give extra unplanned noises.

Pulse

This is the heartbeat of the song. Sing the song or say the rhyme and gently pat your knees or your 'heart' to show how the pulse is steady and regular. Add an instrument eg a drum. At this young age, the pulse should be felt first (rather than heard) so bounce very young children on your knee, or rock them. As they become older actions are great and later clapping and walking or playing an instrument will be easier.

Phrase

As the children develop their singing voices, encourage them to sing each phrase in one breath. Encourage a gentle and smooth singing sound too – eg sing to a sleepy teddy.

Pitch (higher/lower)

This is the height of the notes. Encourage the children to match the pitch. Individual singing works well for this target.

Tempo (faster/slower)

Find songs about things that move (eg animals or transport) – change the tempo.

Dynamics (louder/quieter)

Sing songs in different ways. Invite a child to change the dynamics. Don't let 'louder' become 'shouting'.

Timbre

This is the quality module of sound. It links perfectly with early phonics work – listening to sounds and describing them is a useful activity. It works in singing too - when you play a game like Doggie, doggie (page 63) it will help to build up this skill. The child will hear the timbre of a voice and recognise it!

Listening material tracks

66	SCHUBERT: Wiegenlied (Cradle Song)	2.07
67	BRAHMS: Lullaby, Op. 49, No. 4	2.11
68	BRATTON: The Teddy Bears' Picnic	3.31
69	TCHAIKOVSKY: The Nutcracker, Op. 71a, Dance of the Sugar-Plum Fairy	1.48
70	ANDERSON: The Typewriter	1.50
71	STRAUSS: Pizzicato Polka	2.57
72	FUCIK: Einzug der Gladiatoren (The Entry of the Gladiators), Op. 68, "Triumph March"	2.59
73	JESSEL: Parade of the Tin Soldiers	2.51
74	ANDERSON: Horse and Buggy	3.46
75	TCHAIKOVSKY: The Nutcracker, Op. 71a, Russian Dance	1.11
76	TRADITIONAL (AFRICAN): Uyamemza	2.45
77	ANDERSON: The Waltzing Cat	2.57
78	ANDERSON: Plink, Plank, Plunk	2.55
79	BACH: Anna Magdalena's Notebook – Musette	0.54
80	LOESSER: Inchworm	3.17
81	OFFENBACH: Orpheus in the Underworld – Can-Can	2.13
82	BACH: Oboe Concerto in G minor – Largo	2.52

Published by The Voices Foundation
Copyright © The Voices Foundation

'Lucky bag' cards

Print the pictures from the accompanying CD and cut into individual cards. Either make a double-sided copy with the names of the songs, or write on the back of the cards. Laminate them and place in a bag. The children can choose a song by dipping into the bag.

Published by The Voices Foundation
Copyright © The Voices Foundation

Ally bally bee	Allundé or What shall we do when the baby cries?	All the little ducks
Can you dance?	Bye baby bunting	Apples, peaches, pears and plums
Cobbler, cobbler	Clap, clap, clap your hands	Charlie over the ocean

Published by The Voices Foundation
Copyright © The Voices Foundation

113

Down came Andrew	Doggie, doggie	Cuckoo, cherry tree
Five fat sausages	Easter eggs	Early in the morning
Hari coo coo	Going on a picnic	Five little monkeys
Here is the beehive	Here comes a bluebird	Hello, how are you?

115

| Hokey cokey | Hey, hey, look at me | Here sits a mousie
or
Mice, mice, eating up the rice |
I have sounds	Hush little baby	Horsie, horsie
Incey Wincey spider	Ickle ockle, blue bottle	I see you
Jelly on a plate	Jack in the box	It's raining, it's pouring

117

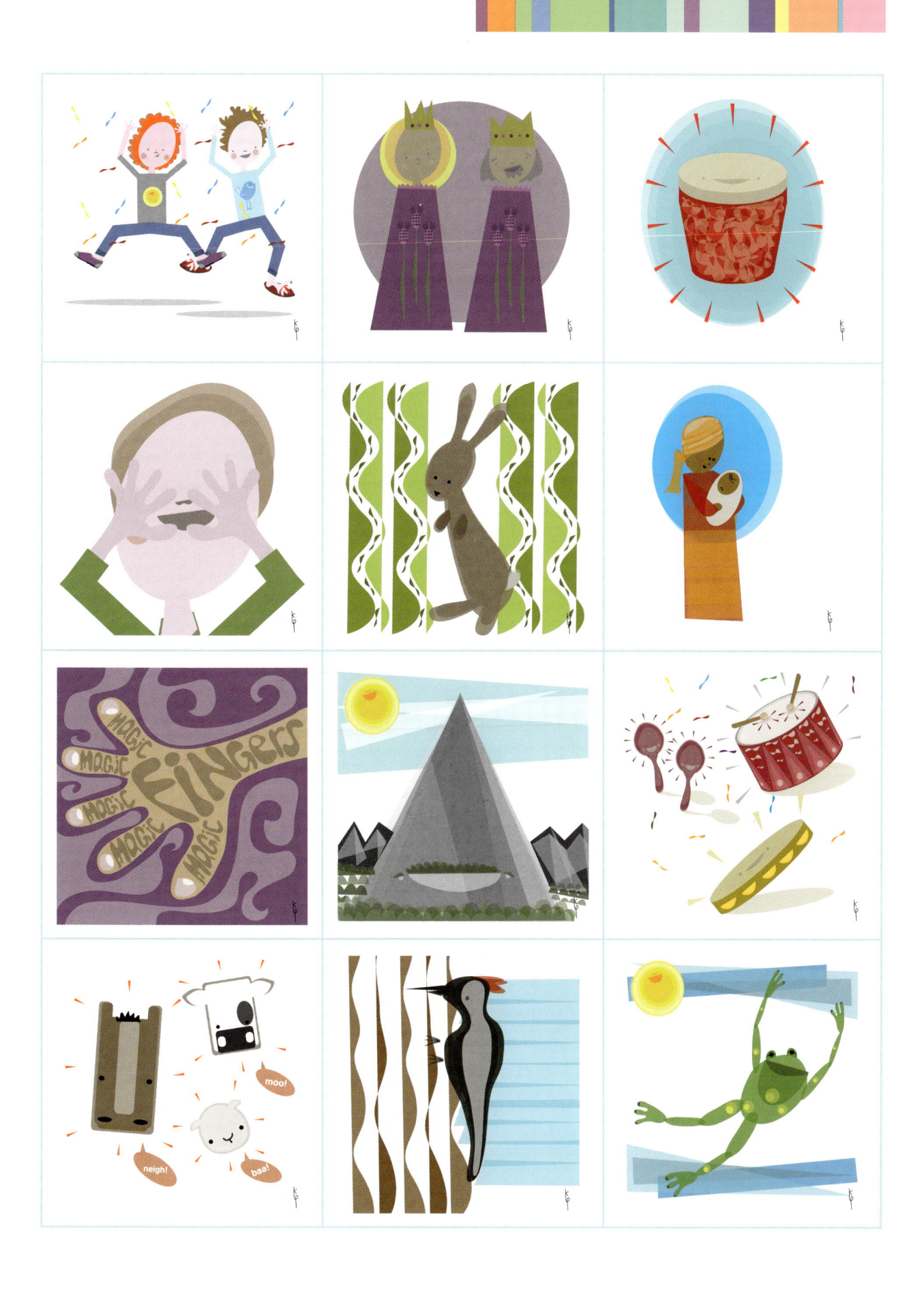

Listen, listen, here I come or The drums in the band	Lavender's blue	Jump, jump, jump Jim Joe
Lullaby my baby	Little bunnies sleeping	Little baby fast asleep
Old MacDonald had a band	Old King Glory	Magic fingers
On a log or The little green frog	Old Mr Woodpecker	Old MacDonald had a farm

119

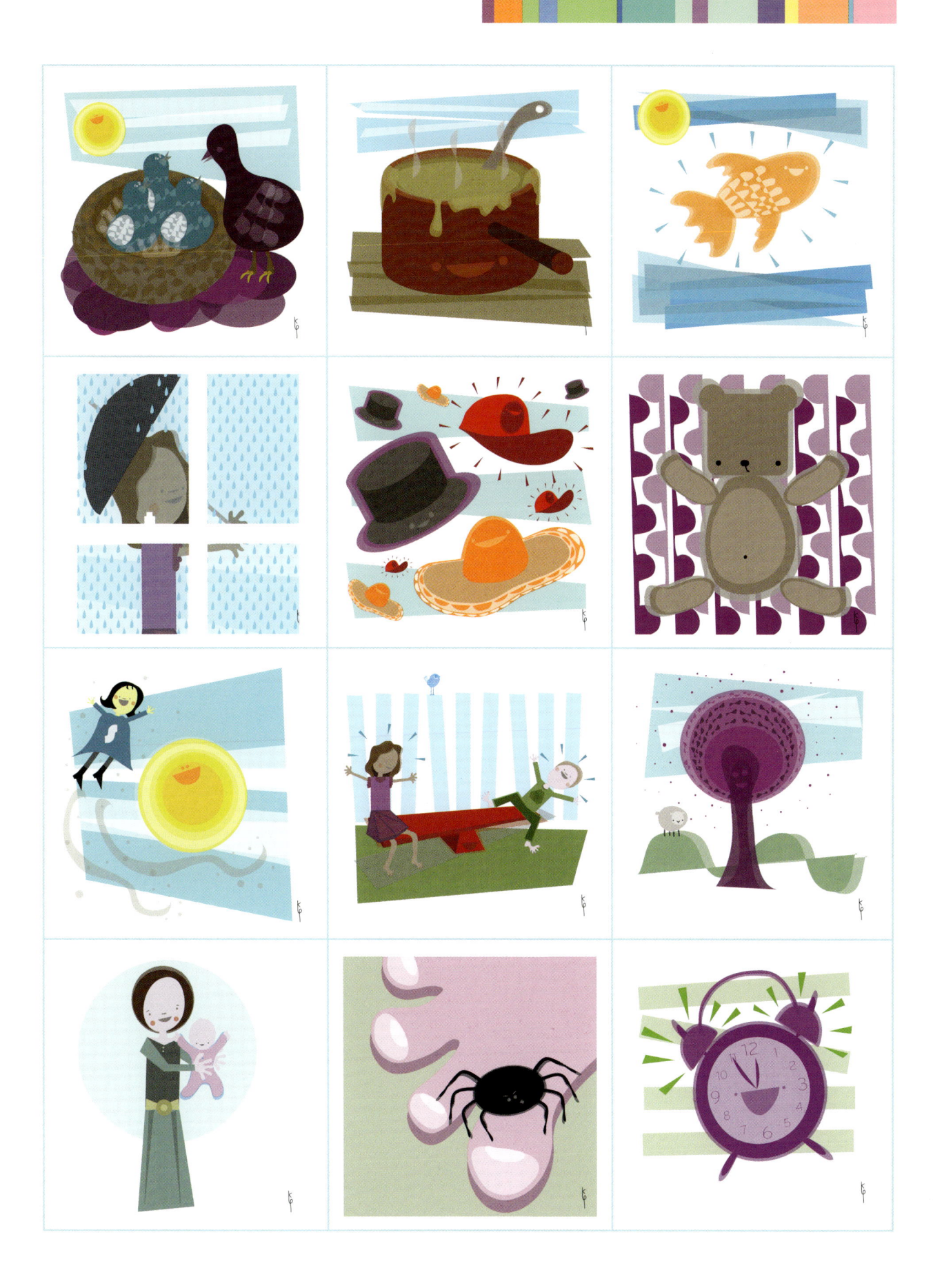

Published by The Voices Foundation
Copyright © The Voices Foundation

Penny on the water	Pease pudding hot	Over in the meadow or Three little birds
Round and round the garden or Teddy bear, teddy bear	Rat-a-tat-tat	Pitter patter or Rain is falling down
Sleep baby sleep	See saw	Sally go round the sun
Tick tock, tick tock	There's a spider on my toe	Suogân

Published by The Voices Foundation
Copyright © The Voices Foundation

121

Two little dickie birds	Twinkle, twinkle, little star	Touch your shoulders
What shall we play in the children's band?	What shall we do with the lazy baby?	Up like a rocket or Zoom zoom zoom
Where, oh where are all the babies?	Where is Georgie?	What's in the bag?
	You are my sunshine	Witch, witch, fell in a ditch